Dancing Quilts

from STRAIGHT PIECES

DEBBIE BOWLES

American Quilter's Society
P. O. Box 3290 • Paducah, KY 42002-3290
www.AQSquilt.com

Located in Paducah, Kentucky, the American Quilter's Society (AQS) is dedicated to promoting the accomplishments of today's quilters. Through its publications and events, AQS strives to honor today's quiltmakers and their work and to inspire future creativity and innovation in quiltmaking.

EDITOR: TRACEY JOHNSON
TECHNICAL EDITOR: BARBARA SMITH
GRAPHIC DESIGN: ELAINE WILSON
COVER DESIGN: MICHAEL BUCKINGHAM
PHOTOGRAPHY: CHARLES R. LYNCH

Library of Congress Cataloging-in-Publication Data

Bowles, Debbie

    Dancing quilts from straight pieces / Debbie Bowles.

        p. cm.

    ISBN 1-57432-818-2

1. Patchwork--Patterns.   2. Quilting.   3. Patchwork quilts.   I. Title.

    TT835.B635523   2003

       746.46'041--dc21

                        2003007338

Additional copies of this book may be ordered from the American Quilter's Society, PO Box 3290, Paducah, KY 42002-3290; 800-626-5420 (orders only please); or online at www.AQSquilt.com. For all other inquiries, call 270-898-7903.

Dedication

To my sisters,

Julie and Lesa.

We make a great team.

Acknowledgments

Books don't get written nor projects completed without a lot of help along the way. A big thanks to...

the Minneapolis Design Group: Bev, Cheryl, Heide, Kay, Pat, and Sandi. They are still testing, stitching, and critiquing with me, and now Heide even bakes for us;

Rubenstein and Ziff/The Quiltworks, for continued support in all manner of things;

my nonquilting gourmet group, for understanding deadlines and always being interested;

Rick, Ryan, and Kyle, for all the big and small things they do to help me out;

Brenda Leino of Plaid Farm Quilting, for the fabulous machine quilting;

my students in classes everywhere—you always provide inspiration and enthusiasm in every class;

and the many companies that generously provided beautiful fabrics and supplies to use in some of the projects: Bali Fabrics—Princess Mirah Designs, Bold Over Batiks, Fiskars Consumer Products, FreeSpirit Fabrics, Hoffman California Fabrics, Omnigrid, Olfa®, Sulky of America, and Superior Threads.

Contents

Introduction

The first Dancing project was introduced in a pattern from my pattern company, Maple Island Quilts. The oddly shaped segments that made up the quilt rows had a lot of unpredictable movement, so I used the term "dancing" to describe how the segments came down the rows, and "dancer" to be able to talk about each segment in the pattern. I called the sewing technique "overstitching" because the smaller square was stitched over the larger square. It is still a good descriptive term that certainly describes what is done with the segments. It has been fun to develop these designs and see the impact that a small, oddly shaped piece of fabric can have on the design lines of a quilt.

The sewing machine and thread industry have kept pace with the quilt world by manufacturing products that allow us the opportunity for great fun and beautiful artistry. Part of the fun of the dancing projects is being able to use those fancy stitches and threads on small pieces. Because you are working on small squares rather than the whole quilt, it is easy to try out those stitches and combine them with the glorious threads that are also available. Even the lowly zigzag becomes impressive when teamed up with spectacular thread.

Many of these projects could be called "controlled inventive." There is a definite place to begin and a definite place to end, and you control the part in between. Your individual dancers will look different from mine, and they will be different on every block and project that you make. The most fun of the dancer projects is the part each quilter adds. Your inventive and unpredictable dancers will make each project uniquely yours, and the photos of the work of others will give you a feel for some of the possibilities.

chapter one

Dance
Lessons

dancing quilts are created from oddly shaped bits of fabric that dance throughout your quilt. The dancers in these projects are created from fabric squares ironed onto larger squares and sewn, or overstitched, in place. The sewn squares are then cut and reassembled into dancing units.

Because the look of a completed dancer unit is determined by fabric choice, the placement of the dancer on the base, the tilt of the dancer, and final placement of the dancer unit in the project, there are many possible variations for each segment and pattern.

Supplies

♪ Rotary cutting mat, ruler, and rotary cutter with a sharp blade

♪ Fabric scissors

♪ Square acrylic rulers or templates for squaring blocks and dancer units

♪ Sewing machine with zigzag capability

♪ Basic sewing supplies

♪ Lightweight tear-away stabilizer for fancy stitching (optional)

♪ Red or green value finder (optional)

Fabric Selection

For the dancers to show, they must contrast greatly with the base fabric, and in some cases, with any adjacent fabric. The contrast can come from value (light or dark) or color. Fabrics that read almost solid will always showcase the dancer or the base. Prints that have large background spaces may be disappointing when cut because the background may be all that shows on some dancers. It may help to think "accent" when choosing dancers or bases, rather than "blending" or "complementary."

The appearance of the project or block may change dramatically if the value of the base and dancer are reversed. If you are hoping to duplicate the look of one of the photographed quilts, choose the same value for each segment you see in the photo.

Quiltmaking Tips

The following tips and general information relate to the dancing quilt projects, which start on page 19.

Sewing and Pressing

♪ All seam allowances are ¼" wide unless noted, and the project directions provide information for pressing seam allowances.

♪ The outside edges of many dancer units are not on the straight of grain and can be distorted if not handled carefully. Be cautious when pressing these projects. Always lift the iron, and never push and drive while pressing.

♪ For all projects, press seam allowances toward borders or sashing strips.

♪ For units with diagonal seams, you may want to carefully re-press some of the seam allowances in the other direction so you will have opposing allowances when joining blocks together.

Dance Lessons

The process for creating dancing quilts, supporting information, and other tips for the dancing technique are listed here. See the project instructions for information specific to each project.

The Basic Steps

The steps to creating dancing blocks are easily achieved by all quilters. The fun comes in deciding what stitch and threads to use, how much and which way to tilt each dancer, and, of course, what fabrics to choose.

1. Place the small square (the dancer) on the larger square (the base), with both squares right side up and the dancer tilted.

2. Press the base and dancer squares together (Fig. 1–1).

3. Sew the squares together (Fig. 1–2).

4. Cut out the excess fabric from the back, leaving about a ¼" seam allowance along the stitching line (Fig. 1–3). Keep the cut-out for a pieced border or binding or another project.

5. Press firmly, pressing any distortion to the outside edges.

6. Square the sewn piece to the size given in the pattern (Fig. 1–4, page 10).

7. Cut the sewn piece into the dancer units specified in the pattern.

The Tilt

Some patterns call for tilting dancers in both directions (Fig. 1–5, page 10). In some designs, a specific tilt (left or right) is needed for the design. If the instructions say to keep

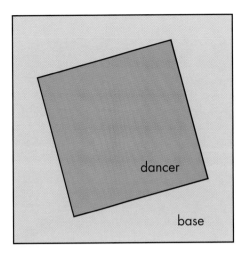

Fig. 1–1. With right sides up, press the two together.

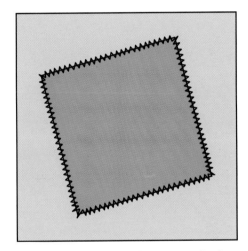

Fig. 1–2. Sew the dancer to the base.

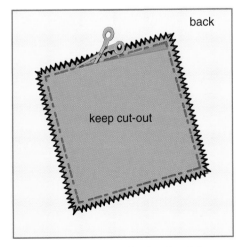

Fig. 1–3. Turn to the back of the sewn square and cut away the excess fabric.

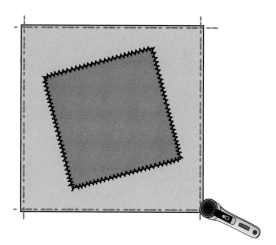

Fig. 1–4. Square the piece to the appropriate size.

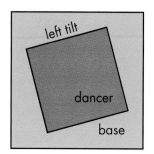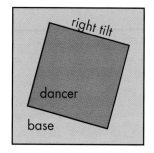

Fig. 1–5. Dancers can tilt to the left or the right.

the tilts separate, you will need both tilts as part of the design. In some projects, you can tilt dancers in both directions just for added fun.

You are never expected to have an identical tilt on all the pieces, and the exact shape of your dancers will change from piece to piece. All of the drawn figures have a generic dancer shape. Your dancers will each be slightly different. They will probably be similar, though, just because there is usually limited space in which to move the dancers. In general, the more tilt, the taller the cut dancer will be. Less tilt will result in a shorter, chunkier dancer.

If the dancer is centered on the base, the cut dancer units will be very similar. If the dancer is off-center, the cut dancer units will be different sizes. Be sure that your dancers are actually dancing and not straight or on point (Fig. 1–6).

Remember that most base squares will be trimmed about ¼" after stitching, and there will be a seam allowance on all the outside edges. Leave at least ½" of base fabric around the dancer. If a dancer square strays into this area, it will be cut off.

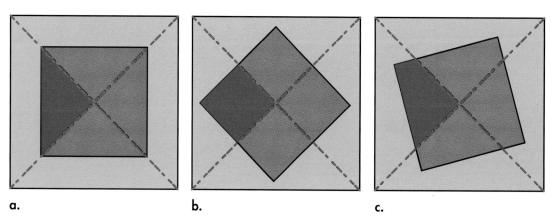

a.   b.   c.

Fig. 1–6. (a) Straight. (b) On point. (c) Dancing.

Sewing the Dancer

It usually is not necessary to pin the dancer to the base. Just pressing them together holds them in place enough to be stacked up and carried to the sewing machine.

Here's where the fun begins. The dancers provide a great spot for decorative stitching. Choose a fancy stitch or zigzag and sew around the edge of the dancer square. If the project will be laundered, choose a stitch that catches the edges of the dancer to prevent fraying. For wall quilts, you need not be so concerned about catching the edges.

Not all the fancy stitches are suitable for the dancers. You will have to experiment with your machine to see which works for you. Some decorative stitches will draw up the fabric quite a bit. These are not suitable for the projects unless you accommodate this by cutting the bases larger. The base squares are always cut about ¼" larger than is needed to allow for some distortion. If you try a stitch that seems to draw the fabric more, cut the base fabrics larger to accommodate this extra shrinkage.

When testing a stitch, notice where to line up the stitch to catch the raw edge, how the stitch goes around the corner of the square, and how the stitch starts and stops. To secure the ends of the stitching line, you can use a backstitch or a locking stitch. Another option is to leave a tail on the thread so it can be threaded onto a needle and stitched through to the back of the piece.

The zigzag stitch is versatile and fast. Changing the width and length creates many variations. Because every sewing machine is different, consult your manual for all the decorative stitches. There are many books available that give detailed information about decorative stitches.

Dance Practice

To Stabilize or Not

Heavily filled decorative stitches will need a piece of stabilizer behind the base square (Fig. 1–7). You can easily determine if stabilizer is needed by trying your stitch on a double layer of fabric for just a few inches. If the fabric bunches up and you want to use that stitch on your dancers, you will need stabilizer. You will want to use a removable stabilizer so that the cut segments of the dancer will be easy to work with. Cut a tear-away stabilizer about the size of the base square and place it on the back of the base square before sewing the dancer.

If you choose a more open stitch, a stabilizer may not be necessary. The double layer of fabric (base and dancer) is adequate for more open stitches like a medium zigzag. A tight, narrow zigzag will benefit from a stabilizer, however.

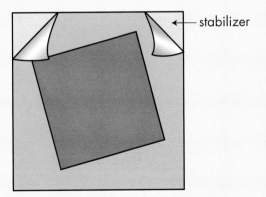

Fig. 1–7. Apply stabilizer to the back of the dancer unit if you are using a dense decorative stitch.

Choosing Threads

In the project quilts, many different threads were used, including monofilament, rayon, cotton, polyester, and metallics. You can have fun choosing a high contrast or blending thread for each dancer. Put those beautiful threads to work for you. You will know if you like a thread only by trying it. Be aware that many decorative stitches can be difficult to remove, so do try out the thread, with the stitch you have chosen, on a doubled fabric scrap as a first step.

Variegated threads are great fun to work with and can function as both an accent or blending thread all on one square. For an interesting treatment, zigzag the dancers with monofilament thread. Then, after the quilt is quilted, go back and stitch a colored thread on top of the monofilament as part of the finish quilting. An ordinary zigzag becomes quite decorative when combined with a fabulous thread.

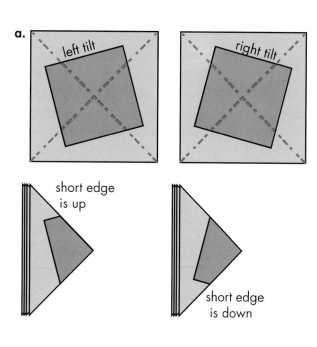

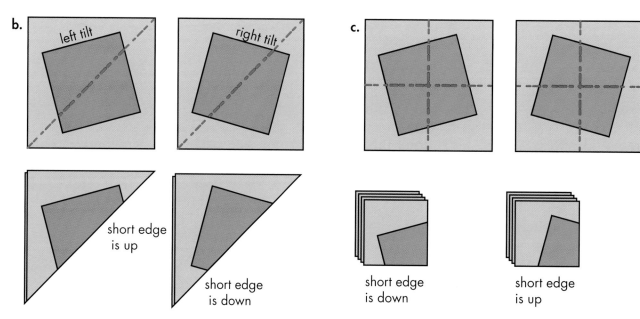

Fig. 1-8. Dancer unit cuts. Pay attention to the position of the short edges in your projects. (a) Quarter-square triangles. (b) Half-square triangles. (c) Squares.

Reducing Bulk

Cut away the excess base fabric from behind the dancer. These cut-outs are used in some of the projects. Work carefully so that you don't cut the dancer by accident. The appliqué scissors with a flat edge on one side work nicely for this cutting. How much seam allowance you leave is not critical. If the dancer is a sheer fabric and the base is dark, you may want to trim as close as you can to the stitching to avoid a shadow.

Pressing the Unit

After stitching, the dancer unit may look a bit ruffled and even misshapen. Press firmly, using steam if desired, and press any distortion to the edges of the square. Because all base squares are cut about ¼" larger than needed, the distortion will be trimmed away.

Squaring the Unit

All patterns begin with a base square that is cut slightly larger than needed, usually about ¼". This extra fabric allows for a bit of distortion during the overstitching or pressing. Most sewn squares are then trimmed to the size given in the pattern before they are cut into dancer units. Each dancer can be trimmed differently. You are not trying to take equal amounts from all sides, and there is usually a very small amount to trim.

Acrylic template squares provide an accurate and efficient method for squaring the sewn dancers. You can use the back of a reversible rotary cutting mat as a work surface. If you are using a template for squaring the pieces, you don't need the lines on the mat.

Cutting Dancer Units

Each sewn dancer will be cut into four squares, four quarter-square triangles, or two half-square triangles, depending on your chosen project (Fig. 1–8, page 12). All of the cut segments from a sewn dancer will be the same. They will have the same slanted angles, and the short edge of the dancer will be in the same place on each segment. The actual shape of the cut dancer will vary; some may be thicker or shorter than others. The angle and position of the short edge will change only if the dancers were tilted in different directions before they were sewn.

Some designs need a specific tilt in a specific place, and the project instructions will tell you to stack the dancer segments into two different piles. Look to see where the short edge of the dancer is. That is the easiest way to determine the orientation of the segment.

Triangle Tips

With so many triangle projects, it may be helpful to study the following information on sewing triangles, both half-square and quarter-square. Success with triangles actually starts when you cut. An improperly cut triangle is not going to behave, and it will not have tidy crisp points no matter how you sew it. Many edges are on the bias so they are easily distorted. Aggressive handling will stretch the triangles before you even have a chance to sew them.

Quarter-Square Triangle Rows

TRIANGLE POINTS. Dancing rows (Fig. 1–9) create a fun, lively, random look. Always try for tidy sharp points, but don't drive yourself crazy. It's the dancers with their odd shapes and angles that viewers will be seeing!

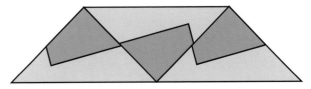

Fig. 1–9. Randomly placed dancers are more lively.

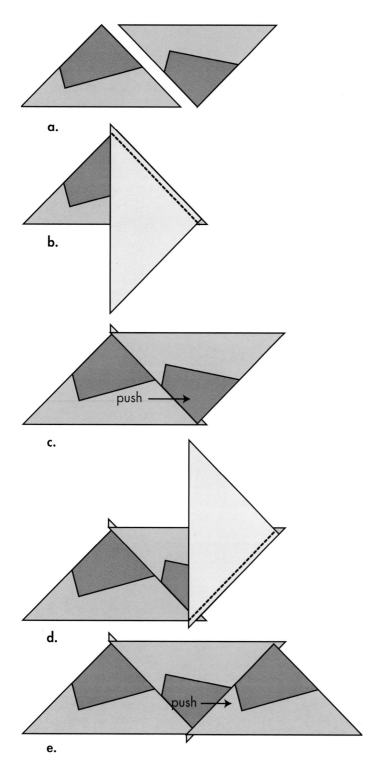

a.

b.

c.

push →

d.

e.

push →

Fig. 1–10. Sewing short rows: (a) Pick up first two triangles in row. (b) Sew together with ¼" seam allowance. (c) Push allowances to one side. (d) Add next triangle. (e) Push allowances to one side. Note that the seam does not always begin or end at the "inside corners."

HANDLING TRIANGLES. Be careful with your triangles. If the triangle tips become frayed, it may be difficult to match the triangles for sewing.

CUT AND SEW CAREFULLY. Because of the bias-cut diagonal edges, a slight variation in cutting or stitching may significantly affect how the triangles go together and how your finished size compares to the size given in the project.

PAPER SAMPLE. To visualize sewing the triangles, try making a paper sample. Cut a 9¼" paper square diagonally twice and draw the ¼" seam allowances around each quarter-square triangle. Position the paper triangles on each other to see where the ideal stitching lines and tips need to be because the alignment changes for the third triangle.

FUDGE FACTOR. For rows of quarter-square triangles that are a bit narrow, each pattern offers an adjoining segment, sash, or strip to absorb inconsistencies and extend the row to the needed width.

SEAM ALLOWANCE. Be sure to use a ¼" seam allowance for each seam line and do not try to start or end all the seams in the "inside corner" that is formed where the triangle tips cross. Depending on the triangle's position in the row, sometimes the seams will land in the inside corner, and sometimes they will not.

SHORT ROWS. For the projects that have only a few triangles sewn together, there will be far less distortion if the seams are not pressed with an iron. Simply use your fingers to push the seam allowances in the direction indicated by the arrows in the project diagram before sewing the next triangle (Fig. 1–10). When all the pieces have been sewn, press from the back to make the seam allowances lie in the correct direction, then turn to the front and press firmly with an up and down motion.

LONG ROWS. For projects that have longer rows of triangles, the strips will be too long to work on without pressing. Sew all the triangles into pairs first and carefully press the seam allowances in the direction indicated in the project diagram (Fig. 1–11). Then join pairs of triangles to complete the row. Press carefully to keep distortion to a minimum.

Half-Square Triangles

To preserve the points of half-square triangle units when they are sewn to other patches or units, sew through the point as shown (Fig. 1–12, page 16).

Adjusting Triangle Row Lengths

No matter how careful you have been, the pieced rows will probably be slightly different in length. Small variations in pressing, the angle of the cut, or the width of the seam allowance can affect the rows. Because it is

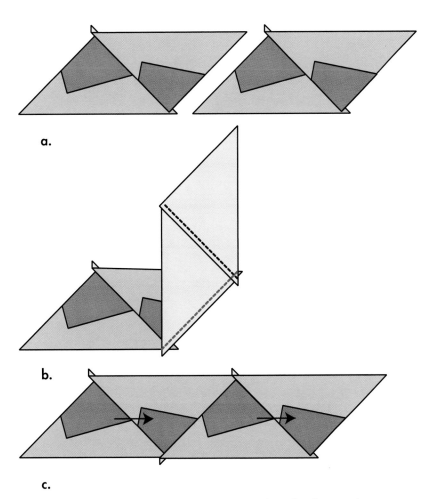

a.

b.

c.

Fig. 1–11. Sewing long rows. (a) Sew triangles into pairs with a ¼" seam allowance. (b) Join pairs of triangles. (c) Press seam allowances to one side.

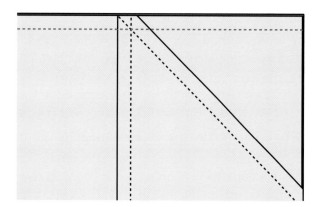

Fig. 1-12. Sew through the point to keep it sharp.

difficult to measure triangle rows if the tips have been distorted, here are two ways to trim the rows to length.

Method A. Do not trim the pieced rows of triangles yet. Add the setting triangles to the top and bottom of each row, then trim the rows to the same length. Note that the setting triangles may be slightly different sizes when trimmed and will not meet perfectly when the border is added. Depending on your point of view, this is fun or awful (Fig. 1–13).

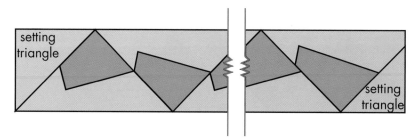

Fig. 1-13. Method A. Add the setting triangles before trimming the rows to length.

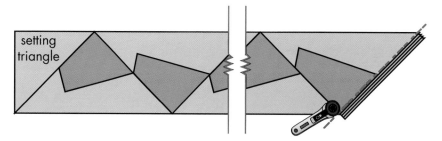

Fig. 1-14. Method B. First, trim the diagonal ends to match the shortest row.

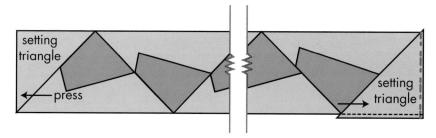

Fig. 1-15. Then, add the setting triangles to the end of the rows and trim again, if necessary.

METHOD **B.** Sew a setting triangle to the top of each row only. After sewing, stack the rows carefully on top of each other, smoothing and aligning the edges. Trim all the diagonal ends to match the shortest row. Cut no more than four rows at a time, aligning the ruler with the diagonal edge that will serve as a template for the cut (Fig. 1–14, page 16).

Sew a setting triangle to the bottom of each row, press the seam allowances toward the setting triangles, and trim off any excess (Fig. 1–15, page 16).

Borders

Before cutting borders to length, always measure your project through the middle horizontally and vertically to determine the proper lengths for your borders. Find the center of your quilt top by measuring and match that to the center of your border strip. Pin generously.

Finishing

When it is completed, place the pieced quilt onto the batting, so the top will stay square until it is time to quilt. To show the quilt top to friends, hold the batting and not the upper edge of the quilt top. Holding the quilt by its edge will result in distortion because the weight of the quilt top pulls on the border seam.

Backing

Cut the panel of backing fabric to the length given in the project instructions. The width of the panel is the width of the fabric, which is assumed to be at least 40".

If two panels are to be cut, they are sewn together then trimmed to the dimensions of the batting. The batting and backing requirements allow at least 2" on all sides of the quilt top.

Binding

The binding requirements are for double-fold binding. The strips are cut selvage to selvage, stitched together end to end, usually with a diagonal seam, pressed in half lengthwise, and sewn to the quilt. It can be fun to create pieced binding from the quilt top remainders.

DANCING IN THE DARK, Shelly Stokes, Miltona, Minnesota. This dramatic hand-dyed fabric was overdyed to achieve the lovely dark shades. The dancers are set off with metallic threads.

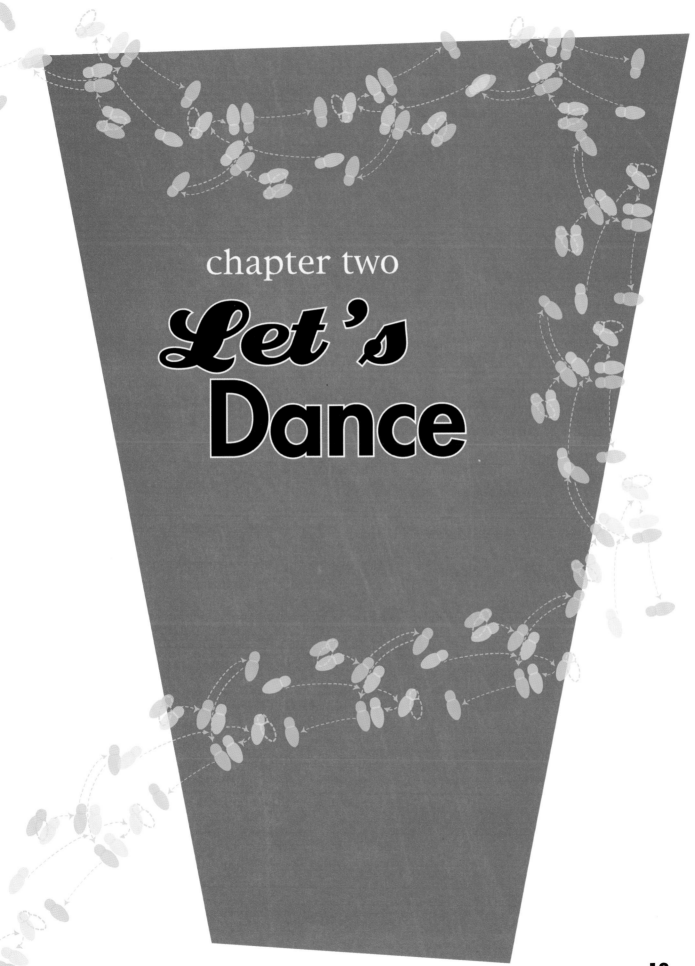

chapter two

Let's Dance

Rock & Roll

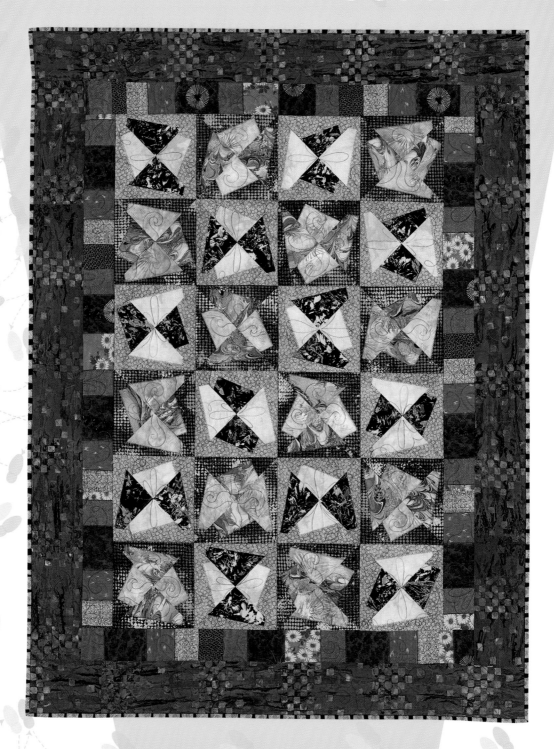

Rock & Roll

Quilt 48" x 64"
24 blocks 8" x 8"

Rock & Roll, by the author; machine quilted by Brenda Leino, Deerwood, Minnesota. For this quilt, the inner border was cut from a striped fabric. It would be easy to duplicate the look by randomly piecing various sized squares and rectangles to make the border strips.

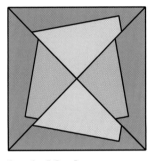
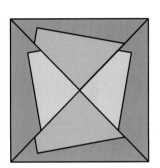

basic block-sets

O nly six fabrics were used in the blocks of this lap-sized project, but each of your blocks will be different because of the tilts and sizes of the dancers. When it's time to join the blocks, you will have even more design choices. It would be fun to do this quilt in a multi-fabric group for a larger size.

This project contains two base fabrics and four dancer fabrics. Base A, dancer B, and dancer C form one block-set. Base D, dancer E, and dancer F form the second block-set.

Yardage

Yardages are based on fabric at least 42" wide.

Fabric	Yards
2 bases	1 each
4 dancers	¼ each*
Inner border	⅝
Outer border	1⅛
Binding	½
Backing	3⅛
Batting	53" x 69"
You can substitute fat quarters.	

Cutting Instructions

Cut strips selvage to selvage.

Fabric	Cut	Cut from strips
Each base	3 strips 9½"	12 squares 9½"
Each dancer	1 strip 7"	3 squares 7" 3 squares 6"
Inner border	5 strips 3½"	
Outer border	6 strips 5½"	
Binding	6 strips 2¼"	
Backing	2 panels 42" x 53"	

Block Assembly

1. Referring to Figure 2–1, make three of each dancer unit, tilting two dancers in each combination one way and the third dancer the other way. Cut the excess base fabric from behind the dancers and press. Trim the units to 9¼" x 9¼". Cut each unit diagonally twice to make quarter-square dancer triangles.

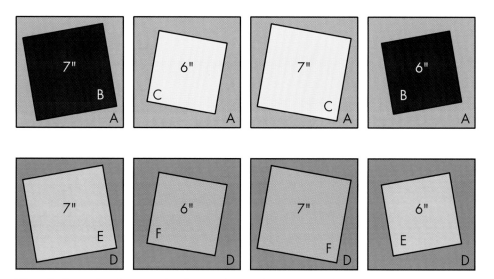

Fig. 2–1. Make three units for each combination, tilting two dancers in one direction and one dancer the other way.

Dance Practice

Tilt Tips

When assembling the blocks, it is easiest to work on one block-set at a time. To get a good mix of tilts, I do my tilting at the ironing board, organizing two of the same-base blocks at a time and pairing the 6" and 7" dancers so that the dancers are tilting different ways in each pair. Remember to allow for trimming and seam allowances when tilting the 7" square. Leave at least ½" of base fabric at all corners.

---

2. For each block-set, organize the quarter-square triangles into groups of four: two 7" dancers and two 6" dancers. Sew the triangles into pairs and the pairs into blocks, pressing the seam allowances as shown by the arrows in Figure 2–2. Make 24 blocks.

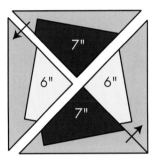

Fig. 2-2. Block assembly. Arrows indicate seam allowance pressing.

Quilt Assembly

3. The quilt top is four blocks by six blocks. Move the blocks around and experiment with row position and rotation. When the blocks are arranged to your liking, sew them together.

4. For the inner border, measure the quilt top and piece the strips as needed to make two side borders. Sew these to the quilt and press the seam allowances toward the border. Repeat for the top and bottom borders. Repeat these instructions for the outer border (Fig.2–3, page 24).

Finishing

5. Layer the quilt top, batting, and backing. Quilt the layers and finish with your favorite binding method. The binding yardage is sufficient for continuous, double-fold binding.

Fig. 2-3. Quilt assembly.

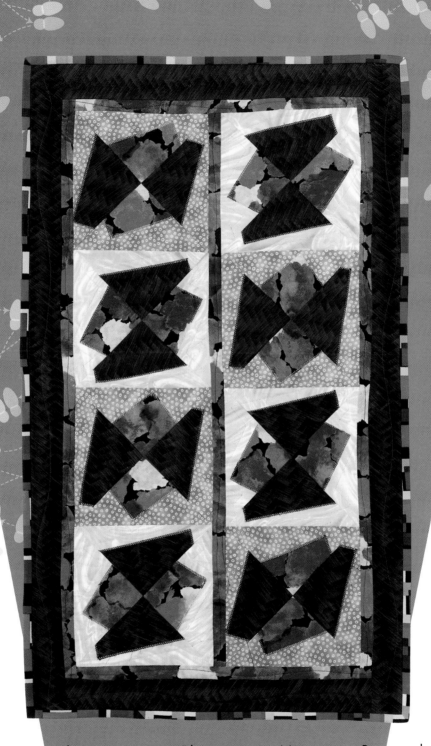

ROCK & ROLL, by Bev Dorsey, Bloomington, Minnesota. Bev made just eight blocks and added narrow sashing to set them off. The center sashing was cut 1¼" wide, the inner border 1½", and the outer border 2½".

Dancing I

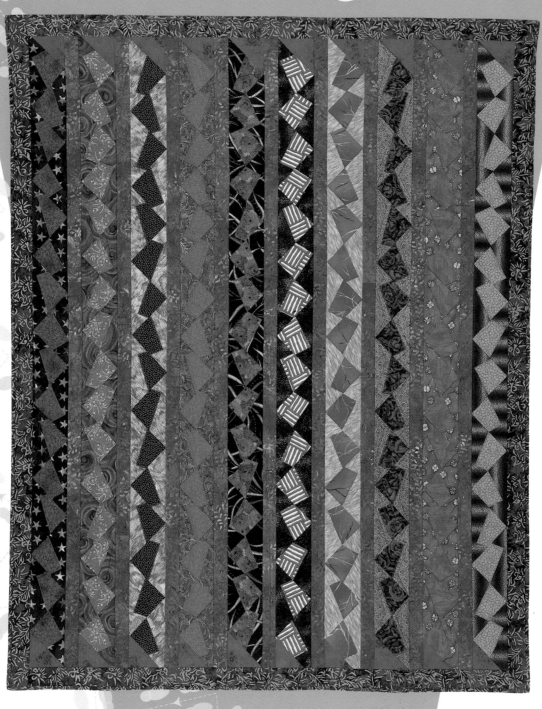

Dancing Quilts from STRAIGHT PIECES – Debbie Bowles

Dancing I

QUILT 57½" X 72"

10 ROWS

DANCING I, by the author; machine quilted by Brenda Leino, Deerwood, Minnesota. This was the first pattern made with the overstitching technique. If you collect color families, this might be a great quilt for you.

Each row in this quilt contains a different pair of fabrics, but it would be fun to design your own look simply by repeating some of the fabric choices or mixing different colors of dancers in each row. The quilt could be made larger with longer rows or more rows and borders. A long strip of triangles could also be used as a valance on drapes, an insert for a long skirt or dress, or the border on a jumper or jacket. As shown in the photo, each row contains one base fabric and one dancer fabric.

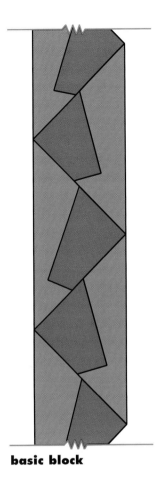

basic block

Yardage

Yardages are based on fabric at least 42" wide.

Fabric	Yards
10 bases	⅜ each
10 dancers	¼ each*
Setting triangles	⅜
Sashing	1¼
Border	¾
Binding**	⅝
Backing	3¾
Batting	63" x 77"

*You can substitute fat quarters.
**If you prefer, binding can be pieced from remainders.

Cutting Instructions

Cut strips selvage to selvage.

Fabric	Cut	Cut from strips
Each base	1 strip 9½"	4 squares 9½"
Each dancer	1 strip 6"	4 squares 6"
Setting triangles	2 strips 5"	10 squares 5"
Sashing	18 strips 2"	
Border	7 strips 2½"	
Binding	7 strips 2¼"	
Backing	2 panels 42" x 63"	

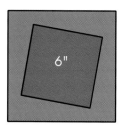 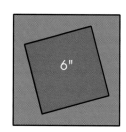

Fig. 2-4. Make four of each dancer and base pair, tilting two dancers in one direction and two in the other.

Dancer Unit Assembly

1. Referring to Figure 2–4, make four of each dancer and base pair for a total of 40 dancer units. Cut the excess base fabric from behind the dancers and press. Trim the units to 9¼" x 9¼". Cut the units diagonally in both directions to make quarter-square triangles. You will need 16 triangles for each vertical row.

Dance Practice

Staying in Line

It is important that the edges be joined as described in Quarter-Square Triangle Rows, page 13, or the row will gradually become slanted. Re-stitch if necessary. Handle gently. These bias edges are easily distorted.

Row Assembly

2. Place dancer units on a design surface and check your dance. Refer to Quarter-Square Triangle Rows on page 13 for sewing long rows of triangles. Sew triangles into pairs (Fig. 2–5). Carefully press the seam allowances to one side, then join the pairs. Continue stitching and pressing until all 16 triangles have been joined in a row.

3. Block the row and trim it to 4½" wide, if necessary. Be careful not to trim off the seam allowances for the triangle points. Repeat these steps for each of the 10 rows.

Quilt Assembly

4. Adjust the triangle row lengths with the method of your choice (pages 15–17). To make the setting triangles, cut the 5" squares in half diagonally. Finish each row with setting triangles on both ends.

5. The instructions for sashing and borders assume a length of 68½". If your pieced rows are a different length, adjust the sashing and borders accordingly . For each sash, join two 1½" strips end to end. Make nine sets. Note the length of your dancing rows and cut the sashing this length.

6. Match the center of a sashing strip to the center of a dancing row and pin generously. If you sew with the sashing underneath the quilt top, you will be able to see the intersections of the diagonal seams. Press seam allowances toward the sashing. Sew the sashing strips and rows together.

7. Piece two side borders the same length as the sashing strips. Sew these to the quilt top.

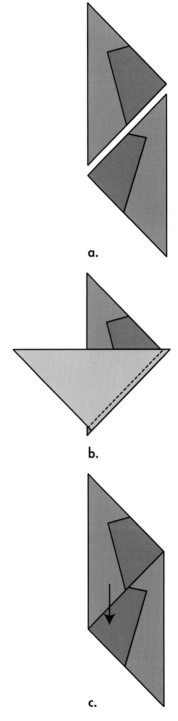

Fig. 2-5. Sewing triangle rows. (a) Starting at one end of a row, pick up the first two triangles. (b) Sew together to make a pair. (c) Press seam allowances in the direction of the arrow.

8. Measure the quilt top through the center from side to side. Piece the top and bottom borders to this length. Sew the borders to the top and bottom edges (Fig. 2–6).

Finishing

9. Layer the quilt top, batting, and backing. Quilt the layers. Piece the binding from remainders or use a different fabric. Use your favorite method to bind the raw edges.

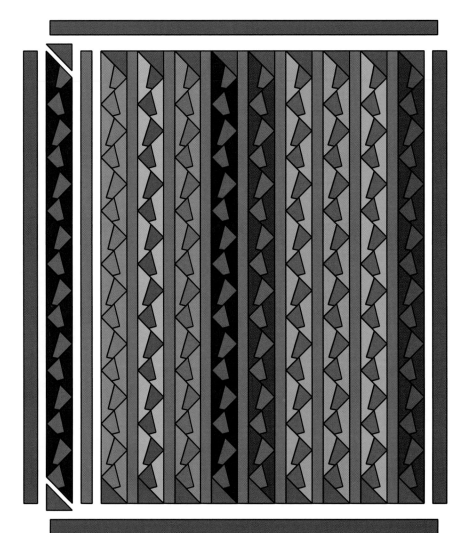

Fig. 2-6. Quilt assembly.

SKY DANCERS, by Lesa Wiedemeier, North Syracuse, New York. Quilted by Brenda Leino, Deerwood, Minnesota. The contrast between the dancers and the bases really makes the rows in this quilt dance.

Dancing II

Dancing II

QUILT 30" X 40"

5 ROWS

DANCING II, by the author. In this smaller version of Dancing I on page 26, some of the fabrics are repeated.

his smaller version of Dancing I can deliver quite a bit of drama if you choose some spectacular hand-dyed, painted, or other unusual fabrics. For a crib-sized quilt, just add a second border. Because you can cut three rows of dancers from one fat quarter, this project provides a good place to use some of those special fabrics you have been saving. Try mixing bits of color in each row. Changing the value of the sashing from blending to high contrast will dramatically impact the look of the quilt. To plan your quilt you need two base squares and two dancer squares for each row.

basic block

Yardage

Yardages are based on fabric at least 42" wide.

Fabric	Yards
3 bases	⅜ each
2 dancers	¼ each*
Setting triangles	¼
Sashing	⅜
Border	⅜
Binding	⅜
Backing	1⅜
Batting	35" x 45"

You can substitute fat quarters.

Cutting Instructions

Cut strips selvage to selvage.

Fabric	Cut	Cut from strips
Each base	1 strip 9½"	2 or 4 squares 9½" (10 squares total)
Each dancer		4 or 6 squares 6" (10 squares total)
Setting triangles	1 strip 5"	5 squares 5"
Sashing	4 strips 2"	
Border	4 strips 2½"	
Binding	4 strips 2¼"	
Backing	1 panel 35" x 45"	

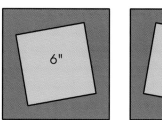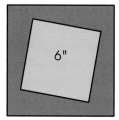

Fig. 2-7. Make two dancer units for each row, tilting one dancer in one direction and one in the other.

Dancer Unit Assembly

1. Referring to Figure 2–7, make two dancer units for each row. Cut the excess fabric from behind the dancers and press. Trim the units to 9¼" x 9¼". Cut the units diagonally in both directions to make quarter-square triangles. You will need eight triangles for each of the five rows.

Dance Practice

Staying in Line

It is important that the edges be joined as described in Quarter-Square Triangle Rows, page 13, or the row will gradually become slanted. Re-stitch if necessary. Handle gently. These bias edges are easily distorted.

Row Assembly

2. Place dancer units on a design surface and check your dance. Refer to Quarter-Square Triangle Rows on page 13 for sewing short rows of triangles. Sew triangles, with right sides together (Fig. 2–8). Gently push the seam allowances to one side. Continue adding triangles until all eight triangles have been joined in a row. Then press the row.

3. Block the row and, if necessary, trim it to 4½" wide. Be careful not to trim off the seam allowances for the triangle points. Repeat these steps for each of the five rows.

Quilt Assembly

4. Adjust the triangle row lengths with the method of your choice (pages 15–17). To make the setting triangles, cut the 5" squares in half diagonally. Finish each row with setting triangles on both ends.

5. The instructions for sashing and side borders assume a length of 36½". If your pieced rows are a different length, adjust the sashing and borders accordingly.

6. Match the center of a sashing strip to the center of a dancing row and pin generously. If you sew with the sashing underneath the quilt top, you will be able to see the intersections of the diagonal seams. Press the seam allowances toward the sashing. Sew the sashing strips and rows together.

7. Cut two side borders the same length as the sashing strips. Sew the side borders to the quilt top.

8. Measure the quilt top through the center from side to side. Cut the top and bottom borders to this length. Sew these borders to the top and bottom edges (Fig. 2–9, page 36).

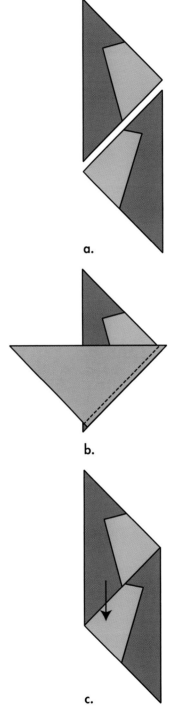

Fig. 2–8. Sewing triangle rows. (a) Starting at the end of a row, pick up the first two triangles. (b) Sew them together. (c) Finger-press as indicated by the arrow.

DANCE LESSONS

Finishing

9. Layer the quilt top, batting, and backing. Quilt the layers. Piece the binding from remainders or use a different fabric. Use your favorite method to bind the raw edges.

Fig. 2-9. Quilt assembly.

DANCING II, by the author. Cheerful garden prints blossom into a bright and lively quilt. This quilt has only one background fabric.

Sash Dance

Sash Dance

QUILT 37" x 37"

4 BLOCKS 16" x 16"

SASH DANCE, by the author. The 8" finished center square provides a great place to showcase something special, such as a photo transfer, redwork, or an orphan block.

Put the quarter-square triangle dancers around a center square, and they become sashing with some unusual angles. You can increase the size of the border to make the piece large enough for a crib quilt. Try some fun juvenile prints for the center square.

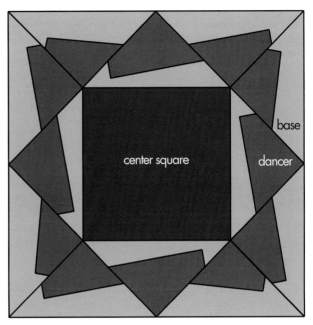

basic block

Yardage

Yardages are based on fabric at least 42" wide.

Fabric	Yards
Center square	⅜
Base	⅞
Dancer	½
Border	⅜
Binding	⅜
Backing	1¼
Batting	42" x 42"

Cutting Instructions

Cut strips selvage to selvage.

Fabric	Cut	Cut from strips
Center square	1 strip 8½"	4 squares 8½"
Base	3 strips 9½"	12 squares 9½"
Dancer	1 strip 7"	4 squares 7" 2 squares 6"
	1 strip 6"	6 squares 6"
Border	4 strips 3"	
Binding	4 strips 2¼"	
Backing	1 panel 42" x 42"	

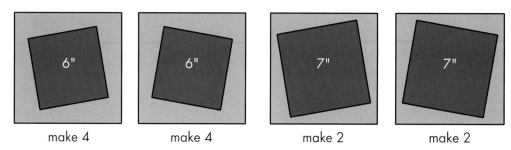

make 4 make 4 make 2 make 2

Fig. 2-10. Make 12 dancer units.

Fig. 2-11. Block assembly. Press seam allowances toward the outside of the block.

Block Assembly

1. Referring to Figure 2–10, make 12 dancer units. Cut the excess base fabric from behind the dancers. Press and trim the units to 9¼" x 9¼".

2. Cut the dancer units diagonally in both directions to make quarter-square triangles. Keeping the units from the 6" and 7" dancers in separate piles, stack together quarter-square triangles with the same tilts.

3. Working with the quarter-square triangles made from 7" dancers, center and sew the triangles to the center square (Fig. 2–11). Notice that the triangle tips extend past the edge of the center square.

4. Sew the 6" dancer triangles into 16 pairs. (Each pair should be made from two different tilts.) Press seam allowances between pairs either way. Center the triangle pairs on the blocks by aligning their seams with the corners of the center squares. Make four blocks.

Quilt Assembly

5. Sew the blocks together in pairs, then join the pairs. Measure the quilt top, cut the side borders to size, and sew them to the sides. Repeat for the top and bottom borders (Fig. 2–12).

Finishing

6. Layer the quilt top, batting, and backing. Quilt the layers and finish with your favorite binding method. The binding yardage is sufficient for continuous, double-fold binding.

Dance Practice

Pressing

When pressing these blocks, use the iron on the seam only. The bias edges of the triangles are easily distorted.

DANCE LESSONS

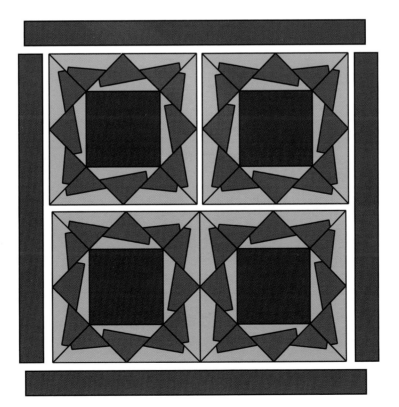

Fig. 2-12. Quilt assembly.

LEAVING HOME, by Heide Burger, Eagan, Minnesota. Heide was deliberate in her tilting and placement, creating four identical blocks.

CHRISTMAS MEMORIES, by Sandra Tundel, Eden Prairie, Minnesota. Sandi filled her centers with photo transfer squares of her children with Santa through the years and cut her border just a bit wider, at 3½".

Double Sash Dance

Double Sash Dance

Quilt 48" x 66"
6 blocks 16" x 16"

Double Sash Dance, by the author. The 7" dancers were tilted both ways when the blocks were constructed, but only one tilt was used on each center square.

In this larger version of Sash Dance, the blocks are sashed again with traditional straight pieces, making each block more distinct. Adding sashing to any favorite set of blocks is a fun way to get a new look.

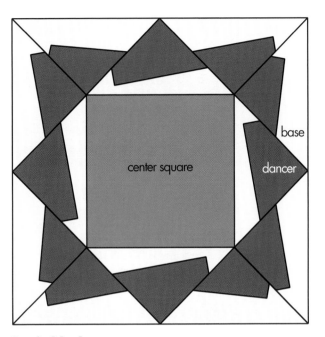

basic block

Yardage
Yardages are based on fabric at least 42" wide.

Fabric	Yards
Center square	⅝
Base	1½
Dancer	⅞
Sashing	¾
Border	1⅛
Binding	½
Backing	3⅛
Batting	53" x 71"

Cutting Instructions

Cut strips selvage to selvage.

Fabric	Cut	Cut from strips
Center square	2 strips 8½"	6 squares 8½"
Base	5 strips 9½"	18 squares 9½"
Dancer	2 strips 6" 1 or 2 strips 7"	12 squares 6" 6 squares 7"
Sashing*	9 strips 2½"	9 pieces 16½" 4 strips 42"
Border	6 strips 5½"	
Binding	6 strips 2¼"	
Backing	2 panels 42" x 53"	

Keep the sashing remainders for the border.

Dance Practice

Pressing

When pressing these blocks, use the iron on the seam only. The bias edges of the triangles are easily distorted.

Block Assembly

1. Referring to Figure 2–13, make 18 dancer units. Cut the excess base fabric from behind the dancers. Press and trim the units to 9¼" x 9¼".

2. Cut the dancer units diagonally in both directions to make quarter-square triangles. Keeping the units from the 6" and 7" dancers separate, stack together quarter-square triangles with the same tilts.

make 6   make 6   make 3   make 3

Fig. 2-13. Make 18 dancer units.

3. Working with the quarter-square triangles made from 7" dancers, center and sew the triangles to the center squares (Fig. 2–14). Notice that the triangle tips extend past the edge of the center squares. Press the seam allowances toward the triangles.

4. Sew the 6" dancer triangles into 24 pairs. (Each pair should be made from two different tilts.) Press seam allowances either way. Center the triangle pairs on the blocks by aligning their seams with the corners of the center squares, then sew. Press seam allowances toward the triangles. Make six blocks.

Quilt Assembly

5. Arrange the six blocks two by three on your design surface. Referring to Figure 2–15, page 48, sew two blocks and three short sashing strips together to make a block row. Press all seam allowances toward the sashing. Make three block rows. Measure the block rows and cut four long sashing strips that length. Join all the block rows and long sashing strips to complete the body of the quilt.

6. Referring again to Figure 2–15, piece 2½" x 5½" sashing remainders into the border strips where desired. Measure the quilt top from side to side, cut the pieced top and bottom border strips to this length, and sew them in place. In the same manner, add the side borders to the quilt.

Finishing

7. Layer the quilt top, batting, and backing. Quilt the layers and finish with your favorite binding method. The binding yardage is sufficient for continuous, double-fold binding.

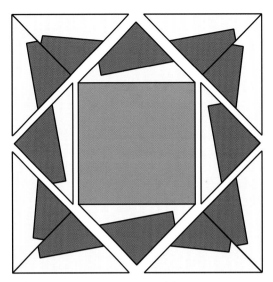

Fig. 2-14. Block assembly.

DANCE LESSONS

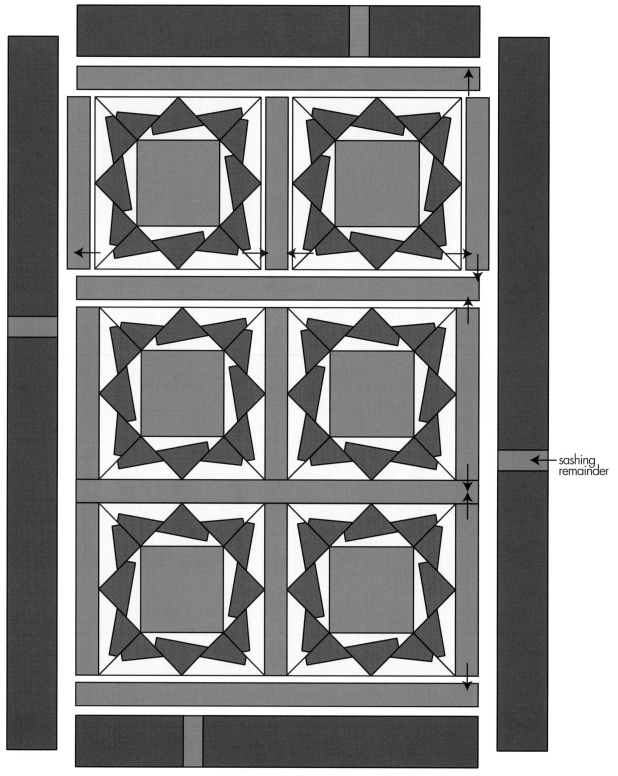

sashing
remainder

Fig. 2-15. Quilt assembly. Press seam allowances as indicated by the arrows.

DOUBLE SASH DANCE, by Cheryl Forsythe, Plymouth, Minnesota. Quilted by Brenda Leino, Deerwood, Minnesota. Cheryl used wider sashing to take advantage of a special border-print motif and decided the quilt didn't need an outer border. The sashing and border were cut 3½" wide.

Cha Cha Zigzag

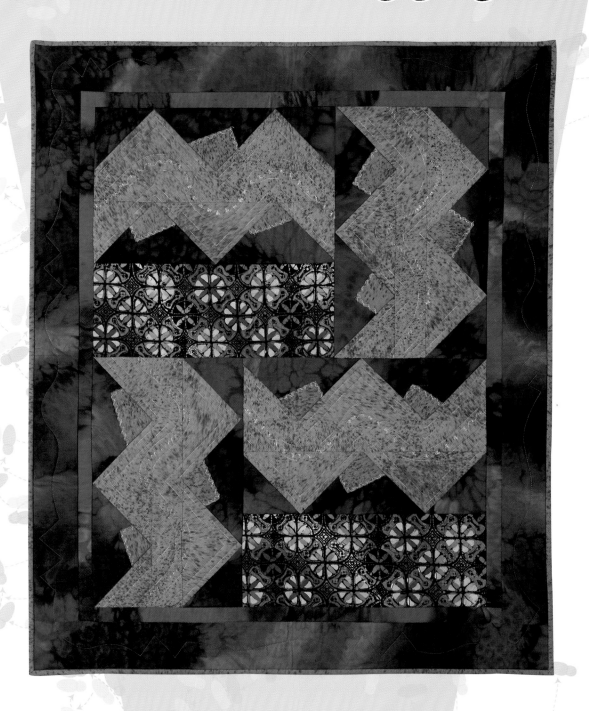

Cha Cha Zigzag

QUILT 34" x 40"

4 BLOCKS 10" x 16"

CHA CHA ZIGZAG, by the author. In these projects, the dancer functions as an accent that is just barely there but gives unexpected interest to a uniform repeated shape.

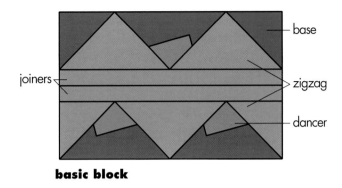

basic block

f perfect points are important to you, precision during cutting and sewing are necessary. However, most viewers will be looking at the dancers rather than the zigzag points. Fabrics with high contrast make the points more visible. The two spacers, which can be made from a fat quarter, provide great places to feature a special fabric.

Note: After this project was completed, the author found that using two joiners simplified construction of this block, so the pattern given here differs in that respect from the quilt in the photograph.

Yardage

Yardages are based on fabric at least 42" wide.

Fabric	Yards
Base	⅜
Dancer	¼*
Zigzag	⅝ (includes joiners)
Spacer	¼*
Inner border	¼
Outer border	½
Binding	⅜
Backing	1⅜
Batting	39" x 45"

*You can substitute a fat quarter.

Cutting Instructions

Cut strips selvage to selvage.

Fabric	Cut	Cut from strips
Base	1 strip 10"	3 squares 9½" 4 squares 5" (end triangles)
Dancer	1 strip 4½"	3 squares 4½"
Zigzag	1 strip 10" 4 strips 2"	3 squares 9¼" 4 squares 5" 8 pieces 2" x 16½" (joiners)
Spacer	1 strip 6½"	2 pieces 6½" x 16½"
Inner border	4 strips 1½"	
Outer border	4 strips 3½"	
Binding	4 strips 2¼"	
Backing	1 panel 39" x 45"	

Fig. 2-16. Make three dancer units, tilting two dancers one way and one dancer the other way.

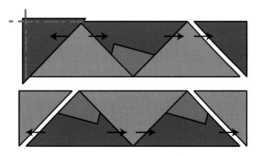

Fig. 2-17. Two zigzag units. Press seam allowances as indicated by arrows.

Block Assembly

1. Referring to Figure 2–16, make three dancer units, tilting two dancers one direction and one dancer the other. Cut the excess base fabric from behind the dancers and press. Trim the units to 9¼" x 9¼". Cut each unit diagonally twice, making 12 dancer triangles.

2. Cut the 9¼" zigzag squares diagonally twice, to make 12 quarter square triangles. Cut the 5" base and 5" zigzag squares once diagonally to make the end triangles. Arrange and sew triangles as shown in Figure 2–17. Make eight zigzag units.

3. Sew a joiner strip to each zigzag unit, as shown in Figure 2–18. Trim each unit to 5½" x 16½". Sew the zigzag-joiner units together in pairs to make the four blocks.

Dance Practice

Joiners

You can trim the joiners to take care of minor inconsistencies in the width of the zigzag units. The important thing is to end up with blocks that are square.

Sew with the zigzag unit on top of the joiner so you can see the triangle points.

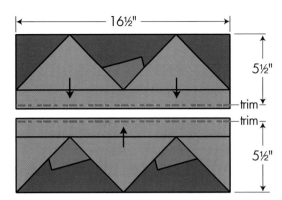

Fig. 2-18. Block assembly. Arrows indicate seam allowance direction for pressing.

4. Sew a spacer to two of the blocks, and press the seam allowances as indicated in Figure 2–19. Trim the block-spacer units, if necessary. They should be 16½" x 16½".

Quilt Assembly

5. Like steps in a lively dance, the pieces can be arranged in different ways. The zigzags are not identical when rotated, so try some new steps to find the arrangement you like best. To make the quilt in the photo, sew the pieces together as shown (Fig. 2–20, page 54).

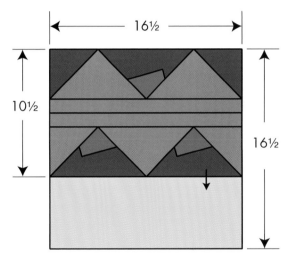

Fig. 2-19. Add spacers and trim if needed. Press seam allowances toward spacers.

Border

6. For the inner border, measure the quilt for the side borders and cut them to length. Sew these to the quilt and press the seam allowances toward the border. Measure across the quilt and cut the top and bottom borders. Sew them to the quilt and press the seam allowances toward the borders. Repeat these instructions for the outer borders.

Finishing

7. Layer the quilt top, batting, and backing. Quilt the layers and finish with your favorite binding method. The binding yardage is sufficient for continuous, double-fold binding.

Fig. 2–20. Quilt assembly.

CHA CHA ZIGZAG, by Beverly Dorsey, Bloomington, Minnesota.
Bev mixed things up by using two different fabrics for the Cha
Cha segments and three dancer fabrics.

Cha Cha Dinner

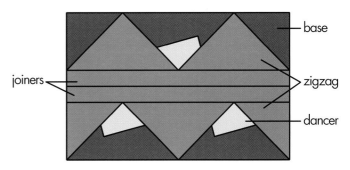

Cha Cha Dinner

FOUR PLACE MATS, 14" x 20"

CHA CHA DINNER place mats, by the author. Repeating the same fabrics in the dancers, bases, and borders gives unity to the set of place mats, while varying the zigzags adds pizzazz.

basic block

(labels: base, zigzag, dancer, joiners)

The zigzag block, which is also used in the Cha Cha Zigzag project on page 50, becomes a set of four place mats in this project. Use the same base and dancer with different zigzag fabrics or put your own spin on the place mats and make them all different by working with a coordinated grouping of fabrics to mix and match. These place mats do not have bound edges. Instead, the raw edges were cut with wave-edged scissors. What a fun way to finish off the edge!

Note: After this project was completed, the author found that using two joiners simplified construction of this block, so the pattern given here differs in that respect from the quilt in the photograph.

Yardage

Yardages are based on fabric at least 42" wide.

Fabric	Yards
Base	⅜
Dancer	¼*
4 zigzags	⅜ each* (includes joiners)
Border	⅝
Binding (optional)	⅝
Backing	1
4 batting pieces	15" x 21"

You can substitute a fat quarter.

Cutting Instructions

Cut strips selvage to selvage.

Fabric	Cut	Cut from strips
Base	1 strip 10"	3 squares 9½" 4 squares 5"
Dancers	1 strip 4½"	3 squares 4½"
Each zigzag	1 square 5" 1 square 9¼"	
each joiner	2 pieces 2" x 16½"	
Border	8 strips 2½"	
Backing	4 pieces 15" x 21"	

Fig. 2-21. Make three dancer units, tilting two dancers one way and one dancer the other way.

Dance Practice

Joiners

Sew with the zigzag unit on top of the joiner so you can see the triangle points.

Place Mat Assembly

1. Referring to Figure 2–21, make three dancer units, tilting two dancers one direction and one dancer the other. Cut the excess base fabric from behind the dancers and press. Trim the units to 9¼" x 9¼". Cut each unit diagonally twice to make 12 dancer triangles.

2. Cut the 5" base and 5" zigzag squares once diagonally to make the end triangles and the 9¼" zigzag squares twice to make 12 quarter-square triangles. Working with one zigzag fabric at a time, arrange and sew the zigzag, dancer, and end triangles as shown in Figure 2–22. Make two zigzag units for each place mat. There will be some extra triangles.

3. Sew a matching joiner strip to each zigzag unit, as shown, and press as indicated by the arrows in Figure 2–23. Trim each unit to 5½" x 16½". Sew the zigzag-joiner units together in pairs to make the place mats.

4. Measure the place mats side to side, cut the top and bottom borders to fit, and sew them in place. Measure the place mats top to bottom, cut the side borders, and sew them in place (Fig. 2–24).

Finishing

5. Layer and quilt the placements. Use monofilament thread and a straight stitch to sew close to the edge around each place mat. Resew a double row of zigzag stitches about ¾" in from the edges. Trim the edges as close to the zigzag stitching as possible with wave-edged fabric scissors.

If you prefer, you can use traditional binding to finish the edges. For double-fold binding, you will need two binding strips 2¼" wide, cut selvage to selvage, for each place mat.

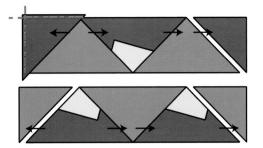

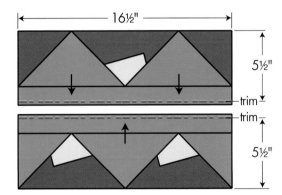

Fig. 2–22. Zigzag unit. Press seam allowances in direction indicated by arrows.

Fig. 2–23. Place mat assembly.

Fig. 2–24. Place mat assembly.

I Could Have Danced All Night

Dancing Quilts from STRAIGHT PIECES – Debbie Bowles

I Could Have Danced All Night

Quilt 64" x 80"

12 blocks 16" x 16"

I COULD HAVE DANCED ALL NIGHT, 64" x 80", by the author. Any multicolored fabric can be used where the striped fabric appears in this quilt.

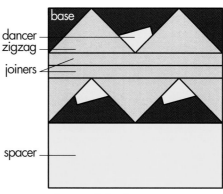
zigzag block

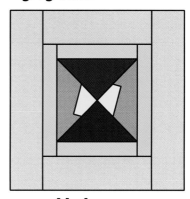
corner block

My sister, Lesa, her daughter, Blair, and I made this quilt for Sarah, the first bride among our cousins. Fabric and instructions flew back and forth from Minnesota to New York. We nearly panicked when we ran out of the striped fabric. By the time more fabric was found, I had redesigned the quilt to accommodate the near disaster.

Yardage

Yardages are based on fabric at least 42" wide.

Fabric tip: The dancer must contrast with the base and the zigzag in all pairs. Choose 4 darks and 4 lights for the 8 fabrics.

Fabric	Yards
8 fabrics (paired for bases and zigzags)	⅜ each
Dancer (includes spacers, inner border)	1⅝
4 accent frames	¼ each*
4 main frames (2 light, 2 dark)	¼ each*
Outer border	1⅝
Binding	⅝
Backing	4⅞
Batting	69" x 85"
*You can substitute fat quarters.	

Cutting Instructions

Cut strips selvage to selvage.

Fabric	Cut	Cut from strips
Each of 8 fabrics	1 strip 9½"	1 square 9½" (base)
		1 square 9¼" (zigzag)
		2 squares 5" (end triangles)
	1 strip 2"	2 pieces 2" x 16½" (joiners)
Dancer	1 strip 4½"	8 squares 4½"
spacer	4 strips 6½"	8 pieces 16½"
inner border	7 strips 2½"	
Outer border	8 strips 6½"	
Binding	8 strips 2¼"	
Backing	2 panels 42" x 85"	

Note: for cutting accent and main frames for the corner blocks, see step 6 on page 65.

Note: After this project was completed, the author found that using two joiners simplified construction of the zigzag block, so the pattern given here differs in that respect from the quilt in the photograph.

Zigzag Block Assembly

1. Refer to Figure 2–25 to make eight dancer units, as follows: Pair each dark fabric with a light fabric. For each fabric pair, tilt one dancer to the left and one to the right. Sew the dancers to the bases. Make eight total.

2. Cut the excess base fabric from behind the dancers and press. Trim the units to 9¼" x 9¼". Cut the units diagonally in both directions to make 32 dancer triangles.

 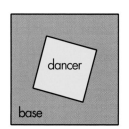

Fig. 2-25. For each pair tilt one dancer to the left and one dancer to the right.

Dance Practice

Getting Organized

Organize zigzag and base fabrics in pairs and work with one pair at a time to decrease cutting and piecing errors. Each pair of fabrics will make two zigzag units with their fabrics in reversed positions. There will be four quarter-square triangles remaining from each pair of fabrics, two dancers and two solids. These triangles will be used to create the four corner blocks. All the spacers and dancers are cut from one fabric.

3. Cut the 5" base and 5" zigzag squares once diagonally to make the end triangles. Cut the 9¼" zigzag squares diagonally twice to make 32 quarter-square triangles. Arrange and sew the zigzag, dancer, and end triangles as shown in Figure 2–26. Make four zigzag units for each pair of fabrics, for a total of 16.

4. Sew a matching joiner strip to each zigzag unit, as shown in Figure. 2–27, and press as indicated by the arrows in the figure. Trim each unit to 5½" x 16½". Sew the zigzag-joiner units together in pairs to make the blocks.

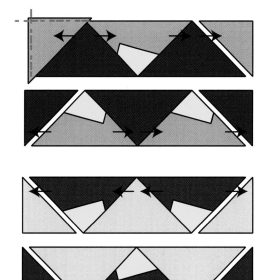

Fig. 2-26. Four zigzag units. Press seam allowances as indicated by the arrows.

Dance Practice

Joiners

You can trim the joiners to take care of minor inconsistencies in the width of the zigzag units. The important thing is to end up with blocks that are square.

Sew with the zigzag unit on top of the joiner so you can see the triangle points.

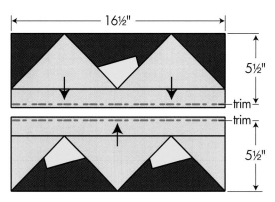

Fig. 2-27. Zigzag block assembly

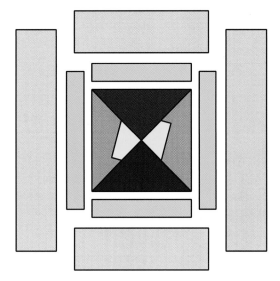

Fig. 2-28. Corner block assembly. Notice in the photo that each block is different.

Corner Block Assembly

5. The centers of the corner blocks are created from the remaining quarter-square triangles, as follows: Organize the triangles into groups of four, with two dancers and two solid triangles for each block: Sew each group of four triangles together. The resulting center squares should measure 8½" x 8½".

Fig. 2-29. Quilt assembly.

6. For the framing strips, select one accent fabric and a light or dark main fabric for each block. Cut the accent fabric strips either 1½" or 2½" wide and the main fabric strips either 2½" or 3½" wide. (The combined frames should measure 4½" wide.)

7. For the inner frame, sew strips to two opposite sides of the block and trim the ends even with the block's edge. Repeat for the opposite sides of the block. Use the same method to add the outer framing strips. Make four framed blocks (Fig. 2–28). Press the seam allowances for all the framing strips toward the outside of the blocks. Square all the blocks to 16½" x 16½".

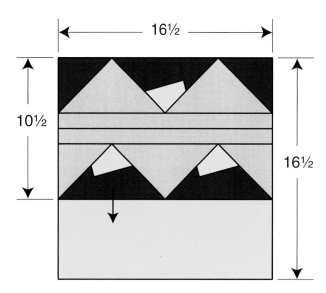

Fig. 2–30. Add spacers, and trim if needed. Press seam allowances toward spacers.

Quilt Assembly

8. Arrange the zigzags, spacers, and corner blocks as shown in Figure 2–29 or create your own layout.

9. Sew a spacer to each zigzag block, and press the seam allowances as indicated in Figure 2–30. Trim the block-spacer units, if necessary. They should be 16½" x 16½". Sew the blocks together in horizontal rows. Then join the rows.

10. Measure the quilt top, cut the inner borders to size, and sew them to the sides of the quilt top. Repeat for the top and bottom borders. Repeat these steps for the outer border, beginning with the top and bottom strips.

Finishing

11. Layer the quilt top, batting, and backing. Quilt the layers and finish with your favorite binding method. The binding yardage is sufficient for continuous, double-fold binding.

I Could Have Danced All Night, by Beverly Dorsey, Bloomington, Minnesota; quilted by Brenda Leino, Deerwood, Minnesota. Bev made her quilt smaller by leaving off the outer border. She used multiple dancers, including some that blend and hide in the zigzag.

Jitterbug

Jitterbug

UILT 48" X 72"

40 BLOCKS 8" X 8"

JITTERBUG, by the author. In this quilt, the base fabric forms the design, and the dancers function as the background. (Quilt shown on page 67.)

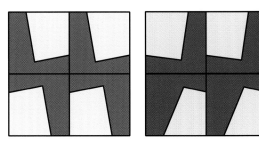

basic block

To duplicate the appearance of the quilt in the photo, be sure to choose dancers that are similar in value and base fabrics that contrast strongly with the dancers. Brenda Leino quilted a large meander with monofilament, then the author quilted over each jitterbug shape with decorative stitches and thread.

Yardage

Yardages are based on fabric at least 42" wide.

Fabric	Yards
10 bases	$\frac{3}{8}$ each
3 dancers	$\frac{1}{2}$ each
Binding	$\frac{5}{8}$
Backing	$3\frac{1}{8}$
Batting	53" x 77"

Note: for the border, use base fabric cut-outs.

Cutting Instructions

Cut strips selvage to selvage.

Fabric	Cut	Cut from strips
Each base	1 strip 9½"	4 squares 9½"
Each dancer	2 strips 6"	7 squares 6" (40 total)
Binding	8 strips 2¼"	
Backing	2 panels 42" x 53"	

Block Assembly

1. Referring to Figure 2–31, make 40 dancer units, tilting 20 dancers one way and 20 the other way. Keep dancers with the same slant stacked together. Cut the excess base fabric from behind the dancers. Save the cut-outs for the borders. Press the dancer units.

2. Use the instructions in Dance Practice: Trimming Units to trim and cut each dancer unit into four 4½" squares. Each set of four quarter-squares will become a block.

Fig. 2–31. Make 40 units, tilting half the dancers to the left and half to the right.

Dance Practice

Trimming Units

When trimming these dancer units, leave as much of the base as possible by doing most of the trimming from the dancer edge, as follows:

♪ Trim the left edge, taking as little as possible to square the edge. From the left trimmed edge, cut a 4½" strip (Fig. 2–32).

♪ Trim the right edge, taking only what is needed to square the edge. Measuring from the right edge, cut a 4½" strip (Fig. 2–33).

♪ Rotate each strip as shown and trim the left edge, taking only what is needed to square the edge. Measuring from the left edge, cut a 4½" square (Fig. 2–34).

♪ Trm the right edge, taking only what is needed to square the edge. Measuring from the right trimmed edge, cut a 4½" square (Fig. 2–35).

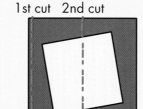

Fig. 2–32. Trim the left edge and cut a 4½" strip.

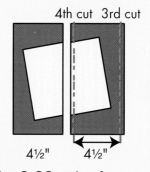

Fig. 2–33. Trim the opposite side and cut a 4½" strip.

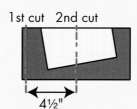

Fig. 2–34. Rotate the strip and trim the left edge. Cut a 4½" square.

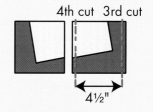

Fig. 2–35. Trim the opposite side and cut a 4½" square.

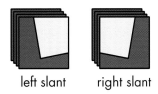

left slant   right slant

Fig. 2–36. Keep the four squares for each block in a separate stack and keep the tilts separate.

left slant segments   right slant segments

a.

Make 2 for each block   Make 2 for each block

b.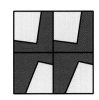

Fig. 2–37. Sew blocks. (a) Join into pairs of the same slant. (b) Two pairs are sewn together for each block.

3. Stack the four 4½" squares from each dancer unit together; they make one block. Keep the tilts separate. For ease of piecing, stack the squares with the dancer in the same corner as shown in Figure 2–36.

4. Refer to Figure 2–37 for the position of the dancers. Sew two pairs for each block. Rotate one of the pairs, then sew them together. Make 20 blocks with a left slant and 20 with a right slant. Press seam allowances any direction.

Quilt Assembly

5. The blocks are arranged five across and eight down. Experiment to find the arrangement that really dances for you. Sew the blocks together in rows, then sew the rows together.

6. The strip-pieced border is created from the base cut-outs and remainders. Sew the cut-outs end to end in groups of four. Press the seam allowances in the same direction. Cut each group into two strips 2½" wide (Fig. 2–38). From the remainders of the 9½" strips, cut strips 2½" wide and any length.

Dance Practice

Bias Steps

The pieced borders are not on the straight of grain and are easily distorted. Handle them carefully and pin well before sewing the borders to the quilt top. You may want to stay-stitch around the edges of these borders to prevent stretching. If someone else will be quilting this project for you, be sure to tell them that the borders are not on the straight of grain.

7. Arrange the border segments around the quilt top and observe the color flow. If you are short of segments, cut 2½" strips from the base fabrics in 5½" lengths.

8. Sew the 2½" border pieces together as needed to make the border strips. Press the seam allowances in either direction. Measure the quilt from top to bottom and cut side borders to fit. Sew the borders to the sides and press the seam allowances toward the borders. Repeat for the top and bottom borders (Fig. 2–39).

Finishing

9. Layer the quilt top, batting, and backing. Quilt the layers and finish with your favorite binding method. The binding yardage is sufficient for continuous, double-fold binding.

If you prefer, you can make pieced binding from all the base fabrics. Cut strips 2½" from each fabric. Randomly cut each strip into two or three segments. Measure the quilt and piece the binding to the length needed.

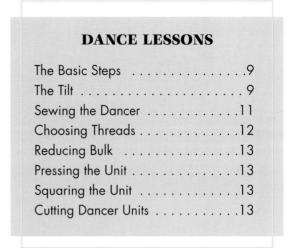

DANCE LESSONS

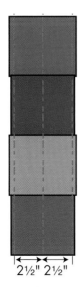

Fig. 2-38. Trim the strip of cut-outs to 5", then cut the strip in half.

Fig. 2-39. Quilt assembly.

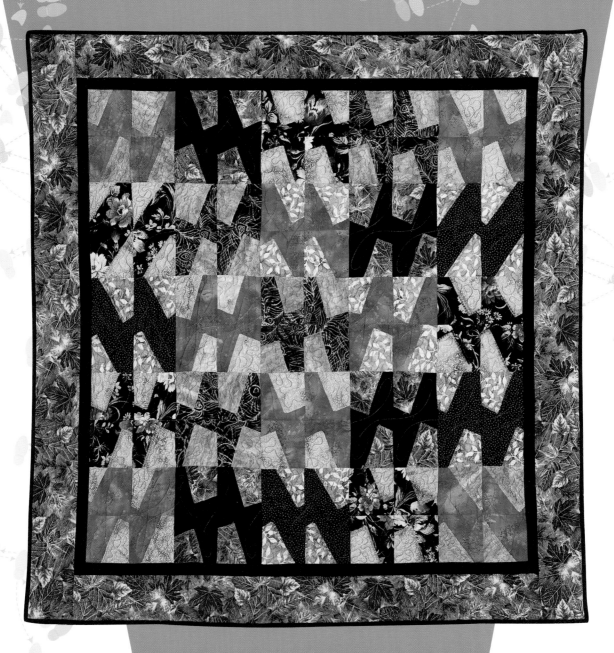

CHOCOLATE COVERED CHERRIES, by Heide Burger, Eagan, Minnesota; machine quilted by Suzanne Ferguson, Mendota Heights, Minnesota. Heide used twenty-five dancer blocks in her favorite pink and brown combination. She set them off with a 1" inner border (cut 1½") and a 4" outer border (cut 4½").

Star Dance

Star Dance

QUILT 60" X 72"
9 BLOCKS 16" X 16"

STAR DANCE, by the author; quilted by Brenda Leino, Deerwood, Minnesota. The addition of dancers to these sawtooth stars makes them more fluid and fanciful.

he dancer tips are positioned randomly for the most movement. You could go to your scrap box for the dancer tips and the random pieced border, and use up to eighteen different fabrics. If you choose reds and greens, this quilt would be festive for Christmas.

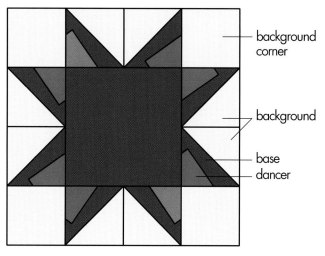

— background corner

— background

— base
— dancer

basic block

Yardage

Yardages are based on fabric at least 42" wide.

Fabric	Yards
Stars	1¾
10 dancers	¼ each*
Background (includes border)	3⅛
Binding	⅝
Backing	3⅞
Batting	65" x 77"
You can substitute fat quarters.	

Cutting Instructions

Cut strips selvage to selvage.

Fabric	Cut	Cut from strips
Stars		
centers	3 strips 8½"	9 squares 8½"
bases	4 strips 7¼"	18 squares 7¼"
Each dancer	1 strip 4½"	2 squares 4½"
border	assorted strips 2½"	
Background		
blocks	4 strips 4½"	36 squares 4½"
	5 strips 5"	36 squares 5"
spacers	5 strips 4½"	9 pieces 4½" x 16½"
border	1 strip 6½"	4 squares 6½"
	7 strips 4½"	
Binding	8 strips 2¼"	
Backing	2 panels 42" x 65"	

Block Assembly

1. Referring to Figure 2–40, make 18 dancer units, tilting half the dancers one way and half the other. You will need two dancers per star. Cut the excess base fabric from behind the dancers and press. Trim the dancer units to 7" x 7".

2. Cut the dancer units diagonally twice to make 72 quarter-square triangles. Cut the 5" background squares diagonally once to make 72 half-square triangles (Fig. 2–41).

3. With right sides together, sew a quarter-square dancer triangle to a half-square background triangle to make a half-square unit. Make 72 units (Fig. 2–42, page 76). Press the seam allowances on half the units toward the dancer and the other half toward the background fabric (keep separate). Square all the units to 4½" x 4½".

Fig. 2–40. Make 18 dancer units, tilting half the dancers to the left and half to the right.

dancer unit   background

Fig. 2–41. Cut dancer units diagonally twice. Cut background squares once.

Dance Practice

Careful Pressing

Pressing is critical with this block. The blocks will usually lie the flattest if the seam allowances are pressed toward the center square. Be aware that you must press carefully to have the blocks finish at the ideal size of 16½". If the finished blocks come up short, try pressing the seam allowances in the other direction.

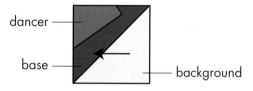

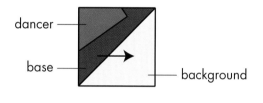

Fig. 2-42. Press the seam allowances in half the units one way and half the other.

4. Sew half-square units, 4½" background squares, and a star center together to make a block, as shown in Figure 2–43. Make 9 blocks.

Quilt Assembly

5. Arrange the blocks and spacers as shown in Figure 2–44, page 77. Sew a spacer to each block. Press the seam allowances toward the spacers. Sew the units in three rows of three. Then sew the rows together.

6. Cut random lengths from the assorted 2½" dancer strips. Arrange the strips around the quilt, alternating them with the 2½" joiner squares, cut from background fabric, to create a look that appeals to you. Begin and end each border strip with a dancer strip. Sew the pieces together to make four border strips.

7. Sew a 4½" wide background border to each pieced border strip. Check the photo for border orientation. Measure the quilt top and cut the side, top, and bottom borders to fit. Sew the side borders to the quilt. Sew 6½" corner squares to both ends of the remaining border strips and sew these borders to the quilt. Press seam allowances toward the border.

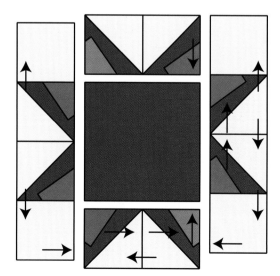

Fig. 2-43. Block assembly. Arrows indicate seam allowance pressing.

Finishing

8. Layer the quilt top, batting, and backing. Quilt the layers and finish with your favorite binding method. The binding yardage is sufficient for continuous, double-fold binding.

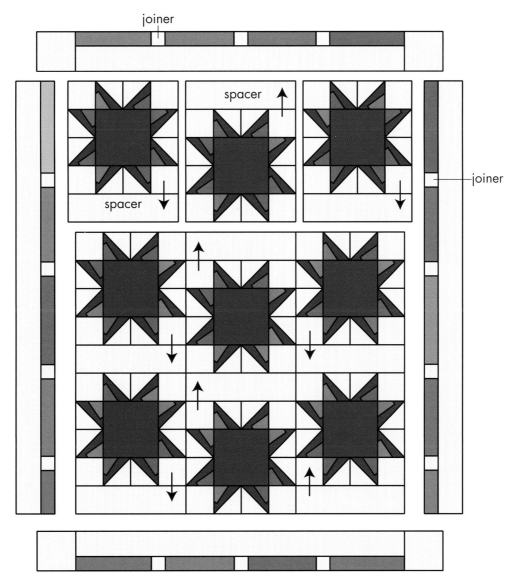

Fig. 2-44. Quilt assembly. The arrows indicate seam allowance pressing.

STAR DANCE, by Cheryl Forsythe, Plymouth, Minnesota. Quilted by Carole Schwankle, Bloomington, Minnesota. Cheryl's quilt really mixed things up: all different star fabrics, one dancer for each star, and spacers from the dancer fabric and a dark background. This is a great example of possibilities.

Grand March

Grand March

QUILT 80" X 104"

16 BLOCKS 16" X 16"

GRAND MARCH, by the author; machine quilted by Brenda Leino, Deerwood, Minnesota. The same sawtooth star blocks from the Star Dance project (page 73) are used to form a dancing border around a pieced center for this project.

Each of the 16 stars has its own dancing fabric. The unfinished center of this quilt is 40½" x 64½". The author challenged the members of her design group to create their own Grand March projects by placing anything they wanted in the center and by using the stars as a border. Hopefully, you too will be inspired to create your very own center for this project, after seeing the possibilities.

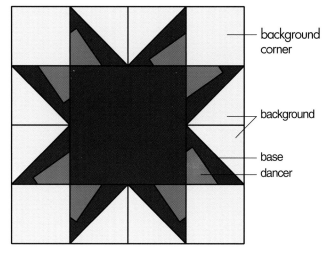

— background corner

— background

— base
— dancer

basic block

Yardage

Yardages are based on fabric at least 42" wide.

Fabric	Yards
Star (includes quilt center)	2⅞
16 dancers (includes quilt center)	¼ each*
Background	4
Quilt center border	¾
Binding	¾
Backing	7
Batting	85" x 109"
* You can substitute fat quarters.	

Cutting Instructions

Cut strips selvage to selvage.

Fabric	Cut	Cut from strips
Star		
bases	7 strips 7¼"	32 squares 7¼"
star centers	4 strips 8½"	16 squares 8½"
quilt center*	1 strip 8½"	3 or 4 squares 8½"
Each dancer		
quilt center*	1 strip 8½"	1 or 2 squares 8½"
and dancers		2 squares 4½"
Background		
blocks	8 strips 5"	64 squares 5"
	8 strips 4½"	64 squares 4½"
spacers	12 strips 4½"	8 pieces 4½" x 20½"
		16 pieces 4½" x 16½"
Center border	5 strips 4½"	
Backing	2 panels 42" x 85"	
Binding	10 strips 2¼" or piece remainders	

*You will need a total of 28 squares for the quilt center.

Block Assembly

1. Referring to Figure 2–45, make 32 dancer units, tilting half the dancers one way and half the other. You will need two dancers per star. Cut the excess base fabric from behind the dancers and press. Trim the dancer units to 7" x 7".

2. Cut the units diagonally twice to make 128 quarter-square triangles. Cut the 5" background squares diagonally once to make 128 half-square triangles (Fig. 2–46, page 82).

Fig. 2–45. Make 32 dancer units, tilting half of the dancers to the left and half to the right.

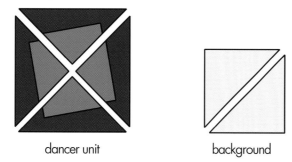

dancer unit   background

Fig. 2–46. Cut dancer units diagonally twice. Cut background squares once.

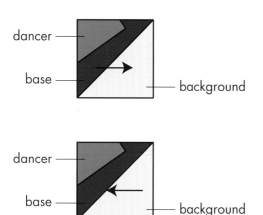

dancer
base
background

dancer
base
background

Fig. 2–47. Press the seam allowances in half the units one way and half the other.

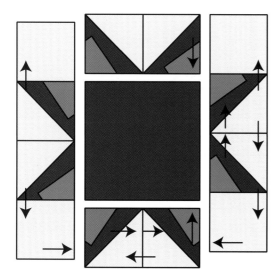

Fig. 2–48. Block assembly. Press seam allowances as indicated by the arrows.

3. With right sides together, sew a quarter-square dancer triangle to a half-square background triangle to make a half-square unit (Fig. 2–47). Make 128 of these. Press the seam allowances on half the units toward the dancer and the other half toward the background fabric (keep separate). Square all the units to 4½" x 4½".

4. Sew half-square units, 4½" background squares, and a star center together to make a block, as shown in Figure 2–48.

Quilt Assembly

5. To assemble the quilt center, sew the 8½" squares together, four across and seven down. Piece the inner border strips as needed, and sew them to the quilt. The quilt center with borders should be 40½" x 64½".

6. Referring to Figure 2–49, arrange the star blocks, the 16½" spacers, and 20½" long spacers around the quilt. Sew the 16½" spacers to each block and press the seam allowances toward the spacers. Join the pieces to make the side border strips and sew them to

---

Dance Practice

Careful Pressing

Pressing is critical with this block. The blocks will usually lie the flattest if the seam allowances are pressed toward the center square. Be aware that you must press carefully to have the blocks finish at the ideal size of 16½". If the finished blocks come up short, try pressing the seam allowances the other direction.

the quilt. Join the remaining stars for the top and bottom borders and sew these to the quilt. Press seam allowances away from the stars.

Finishing

7. Layer the quilt top, batting, and backing. Quilt the layers and finish with your favorite binding method. The binding yardage is sufficient for continuous, double-fold binding. If you prefer, you can make randomly pieced binding from dancing fabric remainders.

Fig. 2-49. Quilt assembly.

GRAND MARCH, by Bev Dorsey, Bloomington, Minnesota; quilted by Brenda Leino, Deerwood, Minnesota. Bev chose shades of red for the dancers and made a bold statement with bright commercial and hand-painted fabrics mixed together.

FLIGHT OF FREEDOM, by Heide Burger, Eagan, Minnesota; quilted by Suzanne Ferguson, Mendota Heights, Minnesota. Heide's quilt is a patriotic salute to the time her husband, Jim, spent in the U.S. Air Force, flying U2s. Her wavy version of the flag was created by using the piecing techniques from Cutting Curves from Straight Pieces (AQS, 2001), also written by Debbie Bowles.

GRAND MARCH, by Sandra Tundel, Eden Prairie, Minnesota. Sandi cut bits and pieces of the star fabrics into the design shapes seen on the fabrics. She fused and machine appliquéd them to the center panel.

Line Dance

Line Dance
QUILT 66" x 82"
63 BLOCKS 8" x8"

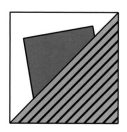

basic blocks

LINE DANCE, by the author. Multiple bases and assorted reds are partnered with five different stripes.

Combining multiple similar bases adds depth and texture to this pattern. These dancers are larger than those in the other patterns because they were created from half-square triangles instead of quarter-square triangles.

Yardage

Yardages are based on fabric at least 42" wide.

Fabric	Yards
Center stripe	⅞
Stripes 1, 2, 4	⅝ each
Stripe 3	⅜
9 bases	⅜ each
10 dancers	¼ each*
Inner border	⅜
Outer border	1¼
Binding	¾
Backing	5
Batting	71" x 87"

* You can substitute fat quarters.

Cutting Instructions

Cut strips selvage to selvage.

Fabric	Cut	Cut from strips
Each base*	1 strip 9¼"	3 squares 9¼"
Each dancer*	1 strip 6"	2 or 3 squares 6"
Inner border	7 strips 1½"	
Outer border	8 strips 4½"	
Binding	8 strips 2¼"	
Backing	2 panels 42" x 87"	

You need a total of 27 base squares and 27 dancer squares.

Cutting Striped Fabrics

Cut strips selvage to selvage.

Fabric	Cut	Cut from strips	Cut diag.	Cut from strips
Center stripe	2 strips 13"	6 squares 13"	twice	24 quarter-square triangles
Stripes 1 and 2	2 strips 9"	7 squares 9"	once	14 half-square triangles
Stripe 3	1 strip 9"	4 squares 9"	once	8 half-square triangles
Stripe 4	2 strips 9"	8 squares 9"	once	16 half-square triangles

Cutting Stripes

Please read all of the following directions before cutting your stripes:

♪ Refer to Figure 2–50, page 90, for stripe placement. For each fabric, use the measurements in the Cutting Striped Fabrics chart on this page.

♪ Cut the squares from the center stripe. Cut each square diagonally twice. The resulting center-stripe triangles are slightly oversized for matching stripes, if desired.

♪ **Note:** The rest of the stripes are cut differently from the center stripe. For stripes 1–4, cut a strip across the fabric, folded just

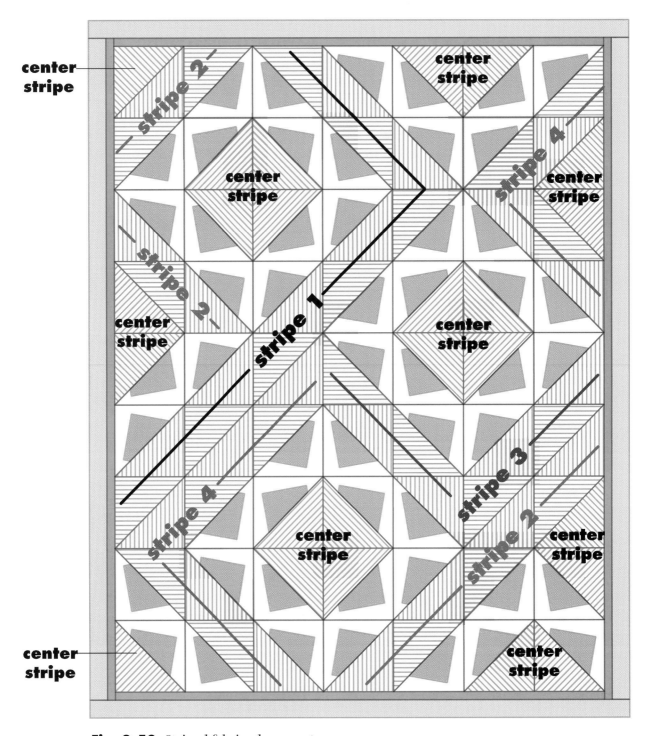

Fig. 2–50. Striped fabric placement.

as it comes from the bolt. Leave the strip folded to cut the squares, then cut the squares diagonally once (Fig. 2–51).

♪Because each strip is folded, the stripes will run in one direction on the top layer of triangles, and in the other direction on the bottom layer (Fig. 2–52).

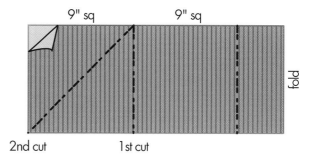

Fig. 2-51. Cut folded strips into squares, then cut squares diagonally once.

Block Assembly

1. Referring to Figure 2–53, make 27 dancer units, tilting half the dancers one way and half the other way. Cut the excess base fabric from behind the dancers and press. Trim the units to 9" x 9". Cut the units diagonally once.

Quilt Assembly

2. Referring back to Figure 2–50 on page 90 or the photo on page 87 as a guide, arrange all of the triangles on a design surface, or set the triangles in an all new way. There will be extra half-square triangles.

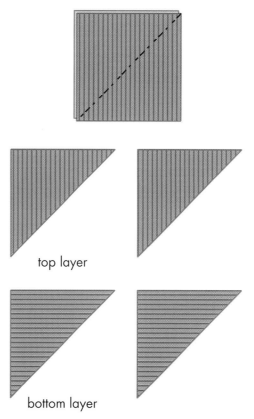

top layer

bottom layer

Fig. 2-52. Cutting squares from a folded strip produces triangles with stripes that run in different directions.

Dance Practice

Joining Unequal Triangles

To sew an oversized center-stripe triangle to a dancer triangle (which is the proper size), align them on their long edges. The larger triangle will stick out beyond the dancer triangle on both short edges.

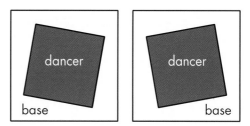

Fig. 2-53. Make 27 units, tilting half the dancers one way and half other way.

Many diagonal seams dance throughout this pattern, making uniform pressing of seam allowances impossible. To simplify quilt assembly, the author has devised the following system:

3. Working across the quilt, one row at a time, mark the left side of each unit with a pin and sew all the diagonal seams. Do not press the seam allowances yet. Just unfold the units and put them back in position on the design surface.

4. Move the side pins to the top of each unit. Working down the first row, stack all the blocks and press all the seam allowances away from the pins.

5. Checking to be sure the diagonal seam in each unit goes from corner to corner, square the units to 8½" x 8½" and return them to the design surface. (All seam allowances are going down.)

6. Stack the second row and press all the seam allowances toward the pins. Square the blocks and return them to the design wall. Repeat the alternate pressing for the rest of the rows. Then sew the blocks of each row together. Sew the rows together.

7. For the inner border, piece strips, end to end, as necessary. Measure the quilt top, cut the top and bottom borders to size, and sew them to the top and bottom edges. Press seam allowances toward the border. Repeat for the side borders. Make the outer borders in the same way (Fig. 2–54).

Finishing

8. Layer the quilt top, batting, and backing. Quilt the layers and finish the edges with your favorite binding method. The binding yardage is sufficient for continuous, double-fold binding.

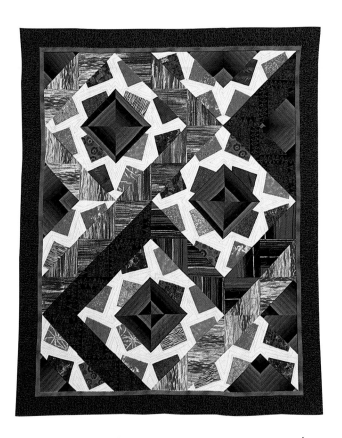

A STASH IS A WONDERFUL THING TO HAVE, by Anna Jones, Rural Retreat, Virginia. The light and dark blues dominate in this version by Anna Jones.

Fig. 2-54. Quilt assembly.

WHY NOT, by Sue Jonas, Wytheville, Virginia, and Anna Jones, Rural Retreat, Virginia. Vibrant colors and strong patterns in the striped fabrics make a bold statement in this quilt.

LINE DANCE IN LIVING COLOR, by Sandra Tundel, Eden Prairie, Minnesota. The irregular wavy line stripe creates very unusual centers. Sandi used fewer base fabrics and chose to make them more contrasting.

Electric Slide

Dancing Quilts from STRAIGHT PIECES – Debbie Bowles

Electric Slide

QUILT 56" x 72"

12 BLOCKS 16" x 16"

ELECTRIC SLIDE, by the author; quilted by Brenda Leino, Deerwood, Minnesota. The striped fabric in this quilt created blocks that all look quite different because the fabric is multicolored with irregular and blurry stripe widths. The dancer functions as the background if you choose a base fabric that blends with the stripe.

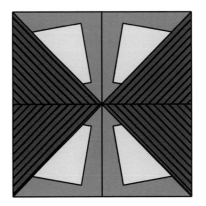

he dancers were controlled by placing the short end toward the center of every block. The stripes were given some order by putting them together in pairs. There are so many wonderful arrangements to consider that you will want to lay your blocks out on a flat surface before deciding how you want to stitch your project.

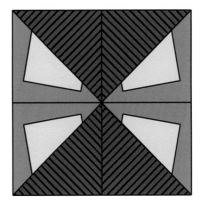

basic blocks

Yardage

Yardages are based on fabric at least 42" wide.

Fabric	Yards
Striped fabric	1⅝
Base	1¾
Dancer	⅞
Border	1
Piping	¼
Binding	⅝
Backing	3½
Batting	61" x 77"

Cutting Instructions

Cut strips selvage to selvage.

Fabric	Cut	Cut from strips
Striped fabric	4 strips 13"	12 squares 13"
Base	6 strips 9¼"	24 squares 9¼"
Dancer	4 strips 6"	24 squares 6"
Border	7 strips 4½"	
Piping	6 strips 1"	
Binding	7 strips 2¼"	
Backing	2 panels 42" x 61"	

Fig. 2–55. Make 24 dancer units, tilting half the dancers one way and half the other way.

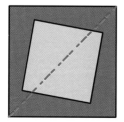

Fig. 2–56. Cut units once diagonally.

Block Assembly

1. Referring to Figure 2–55, make 24 dancer units, tilting half the dancers one way and half the other way. Cut the excess base fabric from behind the dancers and press. Keep dancer units with the same slant stacked together.

2. Trim the units to 9" x 9" and cut them diagonally once, from the lower-left to the upper-right corner (Fig. 2–56).

3. Cut each 13" striped square diagonally twice. The resulting triangles are slightly oversized for matching stripes, if desired. Organize the triangles into two groups, as shown in Figure 2–57.

4. Sew a striped triangle to each dancer triangle to make half-square units (Fig. 2–58). Checking to be sure the diagonal seam in each unit goes from corner to corner, square the units to 8½" x 8½".

Dance Practice

Joining Unequal Triangles

To sew an oversized center-stripe triangle to a dancer triangle (which is the proper size), align them on their long edges. The larger triangle will stick out beyond the dancer triangle on both short edges.

Pressing Seam Allowances

Although it does take a little time, plan for pressing seam allowances in opposite directions. Crisp points are easier to achieve when seam allowances can be "nested" together at seam intersections. Press carefully; many edges are on the bias.

Fig. 2–57. Cut the squares twice diagonally. Stack matching quarter-square triangles together.

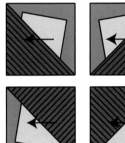

Fig. 2–58. Make 12 of each set. Press seam allowances as indicated by the arrows.

5. Sew the half-square units into groups of two. Check the points after stitching and correct them if needed. Make 12 of each pair (Fig. 2–59). Position the pairs on your design surface, then press seam allowances in opposing directions.

6. Sew the pairs together to make six of block 1 and six of block 2 (Fig. 2–60). Press the seam allowances in alternating directions.

Quilt Assembly

7. Stitch all blocks together as shown in Figure 2–61, page 100. Measure the sides of the quilt top and piece the piping strips to size. Fold the piping strips in half, right side out and press. Baste the piping close to the quilt edge, matching raw edges. Repeat for the top and bottom edges. Sew the side borders in place, over the piping. Repeat for the top and bottom borders.

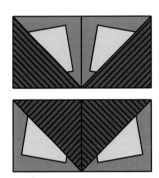

Fig. 2–59. Make 12 of each pair.

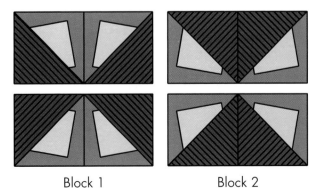

Block 1   Block 2

Fig. 2–60. Block assembly.

Finishing

8. Layer the quilt top, batting, and backing. Quilt the layers and finish with your favorite binding method. The binding yardage is sufficient for continuous, double-fold binding.

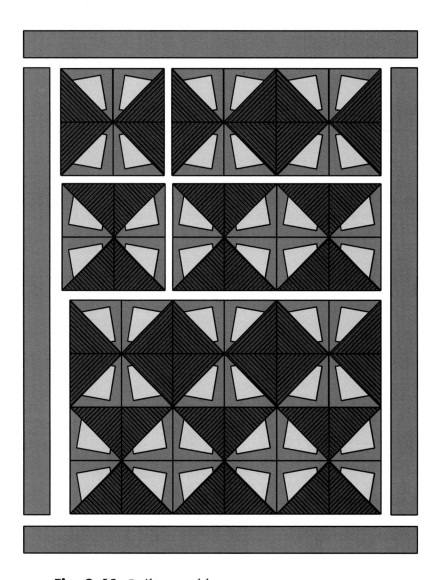

Fig. 2-61. Quilt assembly.

ELECTRIC STORM SLIDE, by Lesa Wedemeier, North Syracuse, New York. Quilted by Brenda Leino, Deerwood, Minnesota. Lesa chose two dancers that had very low contrast with the base fabric and the stripe; then she added two "zinger" dancers and set the blocks in a zigzag pattern. This is a totally different look that is very electric.

Reproducible Planning Sheets

because the look of a project can be so easily changed with value, reproducible planning sheets are included for some projects. These line drawings can be photocopied for use in planning color and value. To preview ideas, color in the line drawings with colored pencils or crayons, paying attention to lights and darks when adding color.

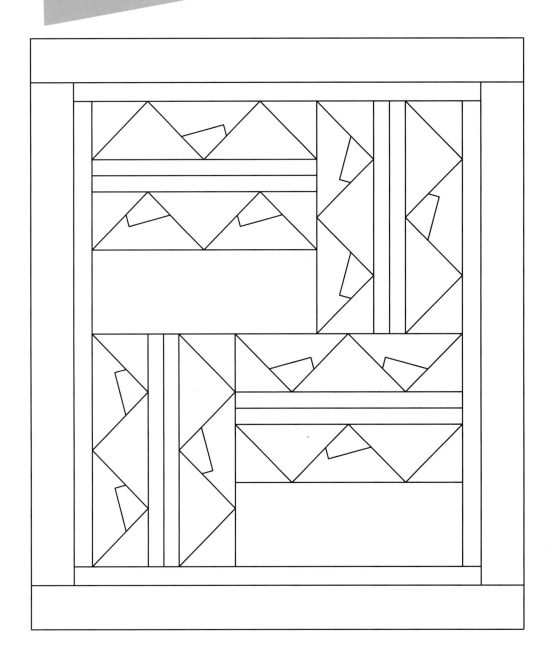

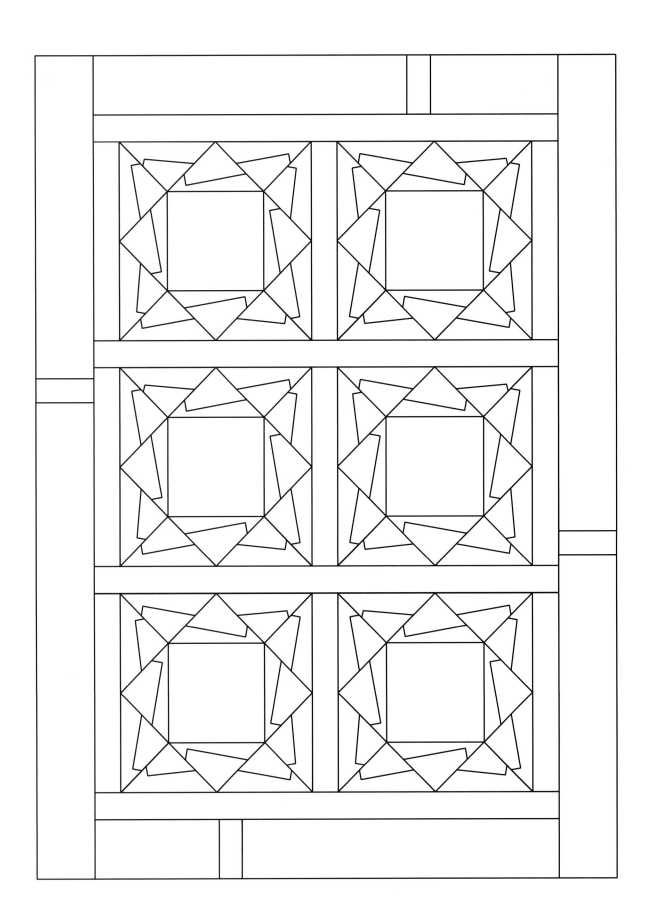

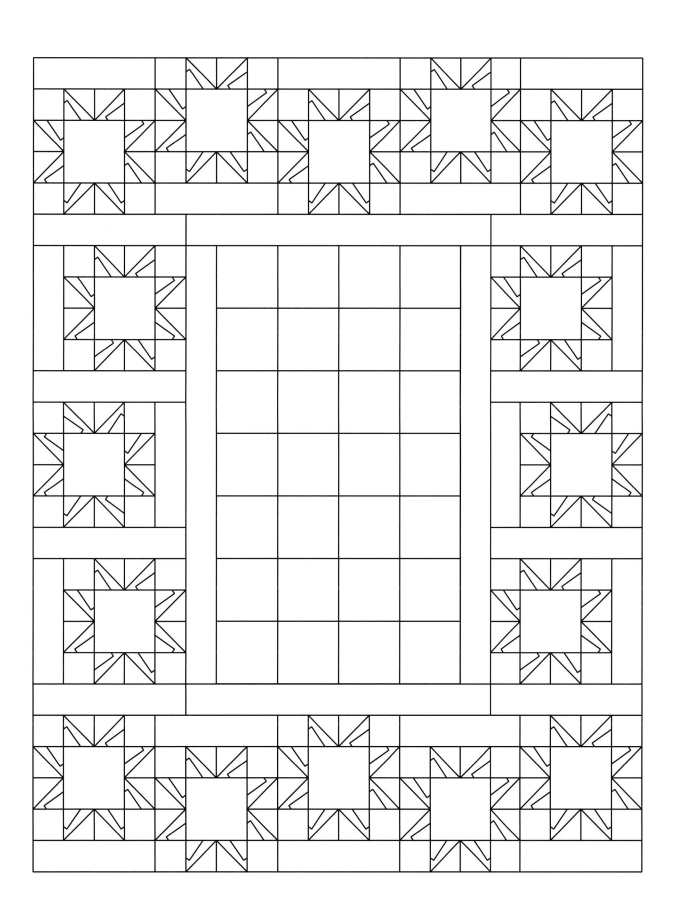

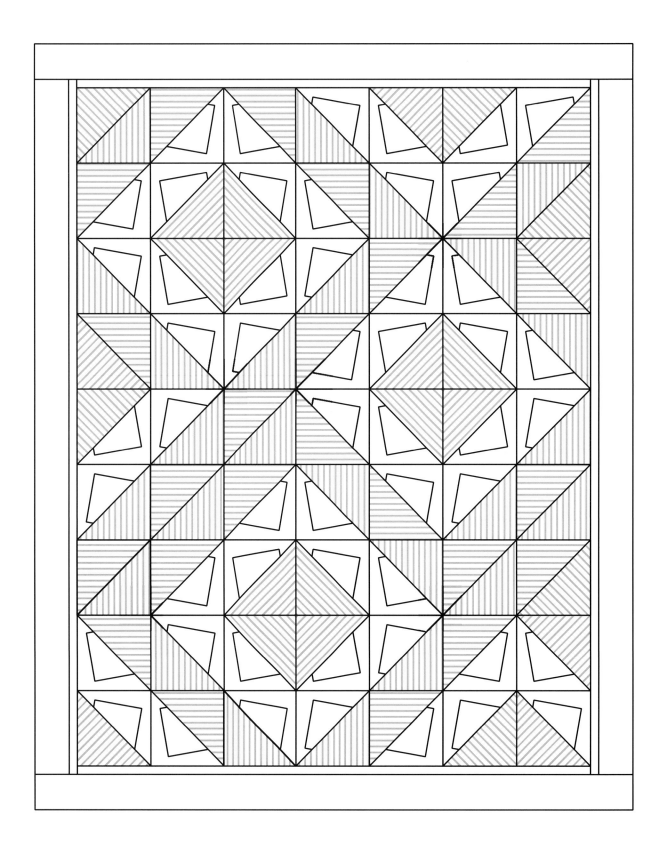

Resources

Hand-dyed, hand-painted fabrics
Bold Over Batiks
(888) 830-7455
www.boldoverbatiks.com
Cha Cha Dinner and Cha Cha Zigzag kits

Cedar Canyon Textiles
(877) 296-9278
www.cedarcanyontextiles.com
Dancing kits

Striped fabrics
Batiks Etcetera and Sew What Fabrics
(800) 228-4573
www.batiks.com

Square acrylic rulers
Leo9 Textiles
P.O. Box 150033
Austin, TX 78715-0033
Phone/fax (512) 472-1655
Email: leo9@texas.net

Patterns, books, and workshops
Maple Island Quilts
Debbie Bowles, owner
www.mapleislandquilts.com
Email: info@mapleislandquilts.com

About the Author

debbie Bowles came to quiltmaking via a lifetime of garment and craft sewing. As an elementary school teacher, Cub Scout den mom, and church volunteer with junior high students, Debbie approaches design, quiltmaking, and teaching as a means of having fun while creating something pleasing to the maker.

Through her pattern company, Maple Island Quilts, she brings delightful designs made with achievable techniques to quilters of many skill levels. Her book, *Cutting Curves from Straight Pieces*, published by the American Quilter's Society, 2001, has opened up the world of curves for many quilters.

Debbie travels nationally to present workshops that are fun and informative. They offer each quilter a space for personal interpretation of the designs. Her home is in Minnesota, where she lives with her husband, Rick, and two sons, Ryan and Kyle.

Other AQS Books

This is only a small selection of the books available from the American Quilter's Society. AQS books are known worldwide for timely topics, clear writing, beautiful color photos, and accurate illustrations and patterns. The following books are available from your local bookseller, quilt shop, or public library.

#5755   us$21.95

#6074   us$21.95

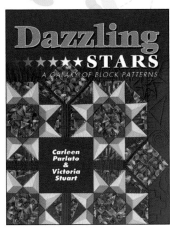

#5844   us$21.95

#6076   us$21.95

#5855   us$22.95

#6079   us$21.95

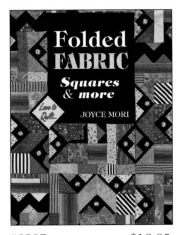

#6207   us$16.95

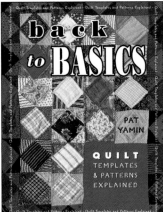

#6293   us$24.95

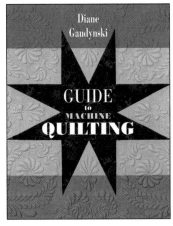

#6070   us$24.95

LOOK for these books nationally, **CALL** or **VISIT** our website at www.AQSquilt.com

1-800-626-5420